Green Gold

SALES SUCCESS GUIDE FOR THE
LEGAL CANNABIS INDUSTRY

Benjamin Richardson

For Information: soulhousellc@gmail.com
Cover design by Mario Butterfield @mariobutterfield

ISBN: 978-1-943014-03-3 (paperback)

Paperback published in 2022 by Soul House, LLC
Printed in the United States of America

Dedication

This book is dedicated to my mother and father Kanoena and Samuel Richardson. Without their love support and wisdom, I would not be who I am or where I am today. They taught me that one of the most important steps in achieving your dreams, is in believing that you can even achieve them. My entire life I watched my parents reach into the upper atmospheres of their potential, each time being willing to sacrifice time, sleep, and comfort to achieve them. Their daily example of hard work and consistency laid the foundation for my own work ethic and has transpired into my passion for people and cannabis. Before my mother passed away, she suggested that I write a book about all the tips and tricks I have used to become successful in this growing industry.

This book is for you, from me and my late mother. She gave me the great idea to create such tool. My mother was always passionate about helping people, and though she is gone, through me and this book, she will still change lives- I love you forever and always- baby of the family- Benjamin Richardson.

My amazing parents. What a gift from God. They helped
me purchase my first Cannabis business. I would not
be who I am or where I am today without them. They
have always believed in me and showed me that hard
work truly does pay off. I love you both so much.

Contents

The Breakdown

"If you are born poor, that's not your fault. But if you
die poor, that's your fault"
– Bill Gates

What is one thing the United States Government
values more than human life? *Money*

Cannabis is here to stay, this (LEGAL) multibillion-dollar international industry is where the modern-day American dream lives on. As we reached the end of 2020, there are over 40 countries worldwide that allow cannabis use, either recreationally or medicinally.

I believe it is only a matter of time before we see a global acceptance of the plant's medicinal affinities and begin to see the negative connotations surrounding cannabis trend from harmful to beneficial. The United States road to legalization has been a similar resemblance of the world's growth towards legalization, with each passing year humanity is expanding its understanding of the plant's properties, and similarly so are the countries and states willing to allow cannabis use for their residents.

Since 2015, 2-3 states a year have adopted some type of cannabis reform for their residents, growing the issue within the United States of cannabis being federally classified as a schedule one drug. The federal definition of a schedule one drug is described as drugs or substances that have a high potential for abuse, as well as having no current accepted medical use for treatment in the United States.

FACT- The United States federal government holds the patent on non-psychoactive cannabinoids — including CBD, to treat specific illnesses.

FACT- Cocaine is a Schedule Two drug that federally licensed Pharmacists can prescribe to patients.

Each year more evidence is unveiled that points to the efficacy of cannabis as a helpful and less addictive treatment for a multitude of ailments, and each year we grow closer to cannabis being set free from the demonized definition placed on it in the 1930s. Currently, 12 states and Washington D.C provide a recreational cannabis industry to its residents, along with 35 states that provide a medicinal cannabis program (must have doctor approval and state-issued Card). The legal cannabis industry has emerged as one of the fastest-growing industries within the United States and is projected to grow exponentially with an annual growth rate of 14% over the next five years, reaching a nearly $30 billion industry by 2025 (New Frontier Data). U.S cannabis sales are projected to more than quintuple by 2025, at this growth rate the United States flaunts the capacity to become the largest cannabis market in the world (Motley Fool). Currently some states are reporting tax revenue earned from the legal cannabis industry to be in the hundreds of millions, there is no way the federal government will sit back and let this economic stimulus slip by. I believe that with the growing possibility of national legalization and the certainty of more individual states legalizing cannabis recreationally, one can be certain that cannabis sales jobs will start popping up like weeds.

In this book, I will switch between the words weed and cannabis when referring to the plant because I love both as a way to reference the plant. The word weed resonates with me and my beginnings with the plant, being 14 and sneaking around smoking with friends (sorry, Mom), hearing music with a new ear, and discovering the munchies. As I grew in the world of cannabis (Scientific term), so did my respect and passion for all knowledge that is cannabis. Through watching YouTube videos and Google, I learned about our body's endocannabinoid system (ECS) and all the other cannabinoids within the cannabis plant.

FACT- The other cannabinoids and terpenes found in cannabis have a greater impact on your high as it pertains to your body and mind than THC. Some of the other cannabinoids and terpenes present in cannabis plants are as listed- cannabinoids- CBN, CBG, CBD, THCA, THCV, and some of the terpenes found in the cannabis plant are- linalool, myrcene, beta-caryophyllene, limonene. If you have never heard of these Cannabinoids or terpenes, you should look them up as you have already experienced most of these terpenes through fruits and vegetables.

My background with selling weed began when I was 18 in the black market of Arizona, this was when I fell in love with the overall job requirements for being a weed salesman.

1. Be friendly, and call people to tell them what weed you have and its price.
2. Work as much or as little as you want.

Selling weed illegally was the first time as an adult that I felt the feeling of making my own money on my own time and overseeing how much money I could make. Fast forward ten years, I have moved to Oregon and was working as a phlebotomist for a plasma center, I quit selling weed as I had become increasingly worried about losing my freedom or getting robbed by one of my customers. At the time I had been working for a plasma collection center for seven years and was climbing the corporate latter faster than anyone I knew in the company, but the unquenchable taste for freedom of time and money was starting to make my blood uneasy. During my time at the Plasma center, I was blessed to meet a lovely couple that owned a medical grow in southern Oregon and allowed me to work for them for FREE! Volunteering at that medical garden is where I planted the seed of passion for cannabis, gaining knowledge, experience, and perspective;

little did I know, I was sprouting the beginning of my legal cannabis career.

If something is your passion, you must be open to doing it for free, especially in the beginning!

"Success in life is always earned, never given"
– The Marines

I have written this book because I have discovered two things, I wish all the people of the world to discover, in your hands you are holding a road map of knowledge and experience that can lead you to a life not yet lived. Through the cultivation of passion for cannabis being mixed with consistent hard work over a short period of time, I have been led me to discover a freedom of time and finances I had never experienced before getting into the industry. Without a college degree, I have purchased a dispensary and wholesale, and processing license, and have made six figures; I am currently working on getting to seven and eight. I am not a special case. Anyone and everyone can achieve what I have achieved, all it takes is a great attitude, persistence, and hard + smart work.

Through this book I will teach you the do's and don'ts that can lead to being successful at selling cannabis in any states' legal cannabis industry. I will teach you tips and sales hacks to help you avoid the mistakes and pitfalls that I have already made. This guide will help you reach your own freedoms much sooner and hopefully with less heartache. More important than the time it takes to reach your financial and time freedoms, is the sustainability and longevity of your success. I believe that all cannabis industries will present similar economic struggles and successes as it is all based on supply and demand. You must learn how to be successful in the season of plenty and season of drought. Funny enough, I prefer the times of drought. Times of drought mean the cannabis supply in the entire market is low, and prices are high; anything and everything is being sold, this is a wonderful period for sales reps with flower to sell. The hard part during the drought is locating the flower. In times of plenty when there is a lot of weed in a market, the sales will be harder because the buyers have more options and are purchasing less frequently; your normal sales avenues will purchase less as more people are coming to them with great deals on flower.

Most states will model their cannabis industry around the successes and failures of the previous legalizing states, adopting some of the same rules and omitting others. One of the most impactful differences between states markets will be how many licenses the state decides to issue, licensure will have a direct effect on the supply in the industry which will translate into sales challenges and opportunities within each state. The sales information and techniques I teach in this book can be correlated with any industry of selling and any state's cannabis Industry, just as Kobe Bryant once said, "The fundamentals that will make you great are the same: persistence, consistency, and self-discipline, you just apply them to your industry".

I am sharing the sale's nuances that I have discovered through visiting 40 + dispensaries a week for four years and being a sales director and mentor.

The only consistency in the cannabis industry is change, new cannabis industries are like iPhones, there will always be updates.

In the cannabis world, we are the ice cream man! They hear us coming down the street, and they come running! Every dispensary needs joints, edibles, cartridges, extracts, and my favorite FLOWER! Sell any of these to dispensaries, and you are selling candy to the candy store. Legal cannabis sales do not require a college degree, a High School diploma or egregious amounts of sales experience. It requires two things hard work and persistence; I came into the industry with nothing but hunger and some charisma. In this book I will show you how I went from making a 5% commission and $1300/ month salary to bringing in $140,000 (pre-tax) in one month-purely selling weed and weed products to dispensaries.

Who is this book for?
This book is for those who want to change their lives and decide they want more out of their lives! More of their own time and more money! This book is for those willing to fall in love with the process, knowing it is a long, lonely, and arduous road and knowing that it will be worth it soon. The tips and knowledge in this book will

give you the freedom to go on a vacation in a split second without having to ask for time off. This book is for those who want the most out of life and are willing to put down the guarantees of a normal 9-5 paycheck and reach for the unlimited earning potential of sales commission checks! #opportunity.

Since being in cannabis sales, my favorite question to be asked is how much do you make an hour? I like this question because it always makes me reflect on how far I've come, as this question has become increasingly difficult to answer because I haven't measured dollars per hour in quite some time. Commissions pay checks will change how fast you see your income grow because there is no cap, it just depends on how little or how much you sell. For example, you can walk into a dispensary and sell a pound of flower for $2000 with a 5% commission rate in 20 minutes or less, and you will have made $100 in 20 minutes, say you do that with 5 shops in one day; then say you were able to do that 20 days out of the month; your commission alone would be upwards of 10k. Now imagine if your commission rate was 10%, I've been paid 15% commission by some companies.

I want to give you this:
Through this book, I will teach you the crucial nuances that I used to carve out my sales success and show you how to emulate that same success in your state. When I turned 25, I began to understand that if you invest in your mind, you can change how you measure earning

your dollars. This book is a compilation of sales tactics I have learned through reading sales books and my personal experiences making sales in the cannabis industry over the last four years. This book is an investment in your mind that will change how you measure earning your dollars.

CHAPTER 1

Getting in the Game

FIRST AND FOREMOST: KNOW HOW to stay compliant with your state's rules! The main difference between the recreational market and the black market is that the police can't arrest us for possession. If you follow the rules set by your state-run cannabis program, you can drive right by the Popo with all kinds of chronic in the car with a smile on your face and peace in your heart.

Before heading out from your office every day, be sure your Ts are crossed, and your I's are dotted! It is not beyond the police to discover you are a cannabis worker while mid-run and then have them interrogate you, if they choose to make your life difficult, they can hold you for several hours. They will be checking for your cannabis permit, checking to see if the route you are on is within the route on your paperwork and be checking over all your product paperwork to see if it covers all the cannabis in your car. I have sold cannabis legally for the last five years and have been pulled over for speeding

1

but have never been searched for cannabis in my car. In Oregon there is no law or rule within our industry that demands that we declare our business to the police, you will want to know if your states have any such requirement.

> *"If you don't know how deep the water is, don't jump in with both feet."*
> – Benjamin Franklin

Before diving headfirst into a sales position with just any cannabis company, you should have some idea of what cannabis products you may enjoy selling. Within the cannabis industry there are flower producers, cartridge companies, edibles companies, extract companies, joint companies and wholesalers. Each company and product require a different sales approach and presents different money-making opportunities. If you are already consumer of cannabis, then think of your favorite way to consume and start there. Sales energy comes from understanding your product and mixing it with passion for that product. The more experience you have with the product, the better your ability to provide valuable insight on how to present it to a buyer. Having previous knowledge on how and why the product is used will give you a palpable excitement surrounding the products you will sell; if you can transfer your energy and excitement about the product you are selling to the intake manager, you can make the sale. Below, I have outlined some of the industry's main cannabis product producing sections, and some of what it takes to sell that product.

Cartridge Company- You will sell the dispensary on the cannabis oil in the cartridge and the technology being used, aka the hardware (just the cartridge piece- without the oil). Knowing the success rate of the cartridge hardware will be a crucial selling point. The purchaser does not want to worry about returns from their pissed-off customers due to leaky cartridges! Beyond hardware, they are going to want to know that your carts are safe and free from any harmful thinning agents. Cartridges produced in the black market that caused a death and some major illnesses were already a national problem and dispensary purchasers will avoid harmful products like avoiding Covid-19! Know what you are selling! There are several ways to produce the oil within carts, as the specific types of oil are made differently and come with different price ranges – you will need to know the prices for Live Rosin carts, RSO carts, Distillate carts, and CO_2 carts. You will look foolish if you come in way overpriced, so make sure you do your market research first.

disciplines. First make sure they **Sales Hack** **Get in and then maintain – Cartridges were some of my favorite cannabis products to sell because once you get on the shelf you can stay there by performing a few accounts never** run out of inventory, Second- give the dispensary value by setting up vendor days, and Third- maintaining and growing relationship with the purchaser.

Edibles Company- Edibles, the most powerful and long-lasting consumer product of all the cannabis products, also comes with the shortest shelf life. Edibles come in all shapes, types, and sizes: chocolates, mints, fruit puree gummies, hard candies, hot sauce, rice crispies and drinks. You will be selling the dispensary on the amazing taste of your edible and how it differs from what they currently sell. Getting samples into the purchaser's hands is an absolute must. They are going to want to taste and feel the effects of your edible. I have noticed that the most appealing edible to the consumer and dispensary purchaser is an edible that is small, cheap, and packs a punch; eating an adult-sized candy bar every time you eat edibles is out of the question. In Oregon, there is an edible company that provides a mini rice crispy that is ("1 x 2") with fifty mg of THC, they are sold to the dispensary at $2.50, and the dispensary sells them at $6 out the door (Includes Tax); every dispensary I work with can't keep them in stock. Edibles can be tricky to sell in volume due to their short shelf life and slow sales speed within dispensaries. In your sales meeting with the intake manager, it will be critical to discuss the shelf life of your company's edibles and your company's process for handling products that reach their shelf life while still on the shelf.

Edible Sales Hack: **Know your shelf life and check on your product often. You don't want the dispensary's customers to be purchasing out of date or moldy products! Too many returns on expired products will get you taken off the shelf.**

Extract Company- Extracts are one of those products that you will need prior background knowledge and experience on before you hit the streets and try to sell. Every day, extract companies are coming out with new ways to produce and create different extracts. Daily technology advances will ensure that extracts become more intricate and eclectic as the industry develops. Due to the connoisseur nature of extracts, you must have more than general knowledge of extracts if you hope to sell it. You will need to know and understand the distillation processes your extractor uses and the solvent used to extract the THC. Whether the extractor uses ethanol, alcohol, butane, propane, CO_2, or is solventless, you must know and partially be able to explain their process. Like flower, the extract's smell, look, and consistency will take you a long way in landing the sale. You must be able to speak to the terpene percentage present in the extract and whether the terpenes were stripped out during the extraction process and then reintroduced, and if the terpenes being used are food grade, plant grade, or cannabis derived. In the extract world, color is everything, the closer your extracts color is to gold, the more appealing they are to dispensaries and consumers. If your extracts come out darker, then hopefully, they come with a scientific reason or a cheap price tag. Having all the information readily available will allow you to present your extracts with confidence and get the sale.

Sales Hack for Extracts sales in the summer: You must beware of the heats ability to affect your product's quality. Extracts are meant to liquify and change consistency when heat is applied. When transported in a warm car, they will potentially liquify/ become soupy. It is imperative that you transport your extracts in a cooler to preserve their form as you go through your sales day in the summer. If you show up to a sales appointment and all your samples have melted into soupy goop, you will not get the sale.

Selling for a flower Producer/ Farm Sales- The flower producer is the heart and soul of the cannabis industry. The rest of the cannabis industry does not exist without it. Selling a farm's flower is how I started in the cannabis industry and selling for multiple farms at one time is how I started a business. Flower is the foundation of all cannabis products. Selling flower for a farm allows you to have at least 3x the opportunities to sell the product, which gives you at least three options to sell elsewhere. You will be able to sell trim and older flower to extractors and cartridge producers. Companies that focus on pre-rolls and edibles are always in the market of purchasing sugar trim and B-bud to make their products. Being a sales rep for a farm is both fun and challenging, you will be given the freedom to make magic happen but will also have a bunch of reporting to do on how you made or will make that magic happen. Flower producers need as much feedback on their flower quality as possible, so they will demand extensive notetaking and reporting on all your sales and sales attempts. Extracting and reporting the correct information is critical to the growth and well-being of the farm and the longevity of your paycheck. Generally, when farms are provided with feedback from dispensaries the farm should be using this information to improve the quality of their finished product, if they have taken your constructive feedback into account, you will be able to see the changes from harvest to harvest. If they don't take your reporting into consideration, you should be worried. Be sure to pay close attention and record the feedback (in the beginning of your sales career, I suggest having pen and paper for taking notes). Here are some examples of feedback you may receive from a dispensary purchaser on the quality of your flower.

- The trim on the buds could be tighter (needs to be trimmed better),
- "This smells like hay," or they say the smell is off (farm may need to work on the curing process),
- There are seeds/seed pods in this flower,
- The THC % is too low for our shop,
- There are a lot of B nugs or shake in this bag (Bags being sold at the highest possible price should be all "A Nug"),

- There is mold or WPM (white powdery mildew) in some of the flower (needs to be discarded, farm needs to check over growing and trimming procedures).

All the above is vital feedback that should be reported back to the farm. In return, it will help the farm produce a higher quality product that purchasers won't be able to resist.

Wholesaler – This is the utility player of the year! Working for a wholesaler will really open your sales game. Wholesalers try to be one-stop shops for the dispensaries they service, often providing their sales force with two or more of the main items produced in the cannabis industry. Wholesalers get to call their own shots; they can sell products for other companies or simply sell their own. These companies create working relationships with flower producers, cartridge producers, joint companies, and extract makers who only want to produce and have nothing to do with the selling headaches of the business. Wholesalers earn their stripes and reputation by having a deep network of relationships and from their ability to move products and get the cash back to the farm ASAP. Their sales model will either be to purchase the product outright and then mark it up to increase the margins or to sell the products on consignment for the specific producer. Depending on how a product producer sets up their company, they might bypass hiring sales reps and delegate the sales responsibilities to a wholesale company that is made up of sales reps.

SALES HACK: Be a giver, samples get you in- Wholesalers usually host multiple types of cannabis products, make sure to set up samples of these products; that's your way in the door. Merely trying to set up appointments where you show them product is not enough. You must give them SAMPLES!! Everyone loves samples and they are more likely to give you their time if they know free samples are coming at the end; plus, if it's a great product and they love the sample, then you should be getting an order very soon!

Just like any job you have ever truly wanted; you will have to put in some extra effort to get a sales position. You will need to SELL them on the fact that you are self-motivated and self-governing, that hiring you is going to make them money!

Finding a cannabis company to work for might seem like a difficult task, and you are sure to have the question.

Where do I start?
Before approaching any cannabis company for employment, I recommend that you have the state-required permit/license/paperwork that allows you to work in your state-run cannabis industry. Showing up to a cannabis company prepared with the correct credentials, will give the first impression that you are a self-starter with common sense; both of those qualities can be hard to find.

I found my first cannabis sales job on Craigslist under (cannabis sales Jobs). The company that I chose required their applicants to send in a two-and-a-half-minute video of why they should pick you as their sales rep. In my video, I told them that I knew a lot about weed, and even more about people; I finished with saying that I was more than confident that I was the guy they were searching for. This flower producer contacted me within two days of my submittal, and after that there were another two interviews: one with the corporate heads and one with the sales director and now mentor and friend Dave. There are many ways to find companies that are looking for sales reps, here is a list of different ways that I have suggested to people.

- Indeed- cannabis Jobs.
- Craigslist- cannabis Sales,
- Visit your local dispensaries and ask bud tenders or intake managers if they know anyone looking for sales reps, look at the farm names or the product names on the shelf, then find them on IG or Facebook, and send a direct message about working for them.
- DM a cannabis company on social media. If you have tried a company's product from your local dispensary and really like it, then I suggest figuring out how to get on their team. Selling products, you like and are familiar with is a major head start in sales.

Thankfully on my initial search I found a cannabis company with great leadership and a focus on growth. Not all cannabis companies will be this way. Some companies will have block head owners who make business decisions that out of touch with the industry and out of touch with the consumers. Some will be doing shady shit that jeopardizes the whole company. I have witnessed large companies crumble due to poor decisions; these were companies that I was sure would-be industry leaders when it all goes federally legal. When you join a company make sure you pay attention to what everyone is doing, especially those calling the shots. You may have to jump ship before it goes down, taking you with it.

CHAPTER 2

No longer a Virgin

DO YOU REMEMBER THE FIRST time you had sex? Just before you engage in this blissful event, you are filled with anxiety, uncertainty, doubt, fear, excitement, and all kinds of happiness. A thunderous flood of emotions sweeps in and overtake your thinking, you instantly become a ball of nervousness because you're not comfortable and unaware of how the hell it's all supposed to go down. Guess what? Cold walking into a dispensary to sell for your first time can bring about the exact same feelings. As soon as you pull into the parking lot, questions produced from fear will flood your mind. What if they laugh at me? What if they don't like my product? What if they ask a question I can't answer? What if they are mad, I came in without an appointment? What if they won't see me? Do I know what to do if they want to buy? Do I know how to close the sale? What if they try and talk me down in price? What if the store gets pregnant? In the beginning of your sales career, all these questions and more will intoxicate your mind every time you pull into the parking lot of a dispensary. The loud voice of fear will try and prevent you from walking in the door. It is vital in the beginning to visit as many dispensaries as you possibly can, as consistently as you can. The only way to get better and more confident is to **Practice!**

In the beginning, you will have the loud inner voice of fear splintering itself into every thought that flows through your mind. With every dispensary that you walk into or think about walking into, that voice will be there. In some way or another, this inner voice will try and talk you out of going into shops, and some days it will succeed. You are striving to become comfortable enough to see new shops as a motivating challenge with endless monetary possibilities. Visualize every new shop as your new highest purchasing shop. What if they started purchasing 50k per month?

You must form a "no man left behind" mindset about dispensaries because, in every parking lot, there will be a battle. The battle will be you vs. your fear voice, and you better show up to fight because the fear bully will be there trying to talk you out of walking in and getting your money. It takes years for this voice to quiet down. The inner fear voice will be in your ear at the beginning, middle, and end of your sales day. In the beginning of your day after you visit three shops, the voice will creep into your mind telling you that you've done enough that day and you should go ahead and head home; in the morning before you leave home the fear voice will try to convince you that sending out emails from home or making phone calls to generate sales is "enough effort" – if they don't reply they don't want to check out my product, right?

WRONG! Get your face into those dispensaries.

Consistently going into your dispensaries has a deep-seated purpose surrounding the most vital aspect of the sales process.

Rapport and Relationship. Having the nerve to walk in random dispensaries is only half the battle. Once you are inside, you must know how to strategically infiltrate the hearts and minds of those who control the dispensary's wallet. Being an expert sales rep means the moment you walk into a dispensary, you are paying attention and noticing every detail that might be brought up in conversation as a opportunity to connect. One of my strongest and most instant connections in this industry came when one of the purchasers from a dispensary shared the same name as my brother. When we first met, I said, "Oh, you have the same name as my brother." He responded, "that's crazy, you have the same name as my brother". We suddenly both recognized that I am Benjamin with a brother named William, and he is William with a brother named Benjamin; I've had consistent sales at his shop for over four years. You can't connect and have immense feelings of joy and sameness through email or a phone call. You must be in person. A sales relationship is a friendship, you must be around that person to nurture and strengthen the friendship. Don't ever make them feel like you are only their friend because they buy from you, you must be genuine in all your interactions. It is up to you to strengthen and nurture that relationship, connect with them on things going on in your daily lives or things you are passionate about outside of cannabis. If you only text or call when trying to sell something, they will feel as if they are being used. Ever had that feeling from someone that you thought was your friend? Are you still friends with that person?

For my first three years as a sales rep for a large farm in Oregon, I visited around 40-60 dispensaries a week, traveling around the entire state. These sales trips would be multi-day where I would either camp at cool locations I discovered or stay in hotels. At this point, I have visited enough dispensaries that I am ready to walk into dispensaries in other states and build national relationships. Having dispensary purchaser friends from NYC to California, what does that paycheck look like? The fact of the matter is that sales is sales, and the only way to generate sales is to hit dispensaries and build relationships. Do the work! Cannabis sales is a numbers game, where if you hit enough dispensaries in earnest, you WILL get sales.

Have you ever practiced anything for an extended period? For hours you practice, getting close sometimes, and other times you ask yourself why are you even trying this? Then it happens. You execute the move or memorize the information flawlessly, and you become filled with power, excitement, and the hunger to do it again. This is cannabis sales. All you need is the first time, that first sale. The endorphins and internal high that transpire from making sales is a very addicting feeling. After the first time, you will chase the opportunity to have that feeling again and again! Can you imagine what it feels like to visit three or four dispensaries in a row and land a sale at each one? Think of the time you felt most confident in life, now multiply that by ten!

There is only way to conjure up this feeling. It's through getting consistent sales, and you only achieve that through building a rapport and relationship with your dispensaries. So, keep your face in those shops!

Sales Hack: You must never lean on emails alone as your invitation to walk into a dispensary. Purchasers are bombarded with emails to the point of anxiety and will just skip over reading most. A successful dispensary owner I know runs a shop and says he gets anywhere from 250-400 emails per day- strictly from vendors! Every cannabis product producer in the entire state contacts every dispensary often.

Sales Hack: Connection points- I have connected with purchasers over so many things. Below are just a few that you can use to relate to your purchaser. Were you both born in the same City? State? Or Birthday? Do they have a unique piece of art in their building? Is the purchaser wearing something that you genuinely like or can relate

to? Do you have a well-behaved dog that you can bring? I bring one of my dogs every day. 99% of my dispensaries not only love my dogs, but now also look forward to seeing them and will ask me why I didn't bring one of them if I ever show up without them. Look for anything that might help you dive into a connection. I don't recommend starting your sales meeting by jumping into your product pitch unless they exclaim, they are very busy and only have time for a short meeting. Only then should you dive right in and look for a way to connect during the pitch.

CHAPTER 3

Show me the Money

ARE YOU READY TO START making money? Like *good* money?
5K- 10k/ Month after taxes, with no college required!
Before the cannabis industry, I had always hunted for
jobs that offered me the highest wage or provided the
fastest opportunity for receiving raises. Never in my life
did I entertain the idea of earning a living via commission. Before the cannabis industry, I worked as an assistant manager and Phlebotomist at a plasma laboratory. I
worked for this company for seven years, chasing the corporate ladder for promotions attached to pay raises. As
an assistant manager at the plasma lab, I earned a salary
of 50k annually, which broke down to about $1500 every
two weeks after taxes, which was not a bad salary, but I
knew I wanted more. Through the cannabis industry, I
have been able to gross 39k in one month, purely through
commission sales with other companies as an owner of a
company the checks have reached well over 100k in a
month. After reading the book "Rich Dad Poor Dad" by

18

Robert Kiyosaki, (which I highly recommend), I learned that making money via dollars per hour is by far the slowest way to make money- game-changing knowledge.

My whole life, I had been afraid to work in sales. What person in their right mind wants to guess if they will be able to pay their bills each month? With any sales position, comes the uncertainty of not knowing how much you might sell each month. How much or how little you sell will directly affect the amount of your paycheck. If this doesn't put some fear in your heart, I don't know what will.

But don't worry, this isn't like selling vacuums door to door, we are selling candy to the candy store, and the candy store always needs candy!

You can and must find sales consistency with your customers, and the key is to earn their trust. You must sell yourself, not your product. You will earn their trust through your customer service and the quality of the product you will bring each time. If you become a master at showing up and building relationships, you will never have to guess if your bills will be paid each month.

The cannabis sales rep has a few options for compensation for your monthly sales. Be sure that you understand your options completely before signing your employee/ general contractor agreement. Getting paid commission in sales is **always** best because earning commission will automatically give you unlimited earning potential. The higher the commission % you can attain at the signing of your contract, the faster your paycheck exponentially grows when the sales start to roll in.

Below I have laid out the earning potential of each payment method I have encountered in the legal cannabis industry. I have been paid cash for flower trimming jobs, commission % only in sales positions, salary only sales positions, and a combination of salary mixed with commissions in a sales position. I will base the following statistics on a meager $50,000 sales month (you can reach this sales goal in a year or less).

What your paycheck can look like after a 50k dollar sales month.

Under the table- Whatever you have agreed to with the company you are working for. There is no tracking of employment, no tracking of wages. You are pretty much a ghost employee. Sometimes legal businesses will pay you this way if they're not planning on having you work for them for too long and feel as if filing the paperwork just isn't worth it.

Salary only/ Based on a 50k annual salary (4,167/ month- before taxes- $1500 every two weeks after taxes. Hopefully, you don't start selling more than 30,000 per month because if you do, you will be making less than you could if you were commission only.

Salary + Commission. When being paid salary and commission, they will usually offer you a lower salary combined with a lower commission. Being paid this method will bring you two pay checks per month. One paycheck, you will receive your salary only, and the other paycheck in the month is salary + commission.

This is safety mixed with opportunity.

When I first started selling for the farm Grown Rogue, they offered me a Salary of 29k a year which breaks down to 1800/month** pre-tax (+ 6% Commission-). Your two pay checks that month will be as follows. 1ST check- salary only, after taxes = $900; Second check of the month is your salary + commission, based on a 50k sales month is $900 + 3000 commission = $3900, after taxes you will take home around $3120. So, in a month, you will earn about 4,000 with taxes taken out. Some companies pay commissions at the end of the month, and some pay commissions on the first paycheck of the next month. Know this before you start!

Commission only – By far my favorite, but it can be extremely tough in the beginning of a new cannabis sales rep career, due to not having previously built account relationships your sales will be slow in the beginning. Earning money via commission only will allow you to obtain a higher commission rate, when you are paid commissions only the company only pays you out based on the sales you land, with money turned in. Essentially you are paying for yourself, and you can land commission rates usually ranging from 10-15%.

$50k sales month – $5,000 (10%) – $7500 (15%) – after you deduct 20% for your taxes- you make $4000 – $5000 take home. Being paid commission only means that taxes are not taken out, you will be employed as a 1099 private contractor. You will be fully paid out to the equivalent of your commission % and must pay your own taxes the following tax year. This is a good and bad thing. Good because you will be receiving large sums of money each month and if used wisely you can use the money to invest and make you more money. Bad because you must personally track how much tax liability is and have a high level of financial discipline to ensure that you save enough money to cover your ensuing tax bill.

The above payment scenarios have their benefits and pitfalls, be sure you understand the pros and cons of being compensated in each scenario. It's okay to start off in a safe salary only position, but the real money is made in the commission's lane. Be aware and notice when your value to the industry raises, as your value raises; so, should your pay checks

Don't ever let anyone cap how much you can earn in one month. Once you start earning large commission checks you will realize that your time is more valuable than you currently think.

Sales Hack: Be aware if you must sign a do not compete. It is very possible that the Cannabis company you get employed by, asks you to sign a do not compete form. For different companies this means different things, some companies will tell you that you can't work for anyone else in the industry, and some companies will tell you that you can't work for a specific type of cannabis company (Ex-If you are hired at a farm, they may say that you can't work for any other farms or sell any other flower but theirs). Make sure you know if you are having to sign a do not compete contract, and if so, what are the limits of the contract?

Sales Hack: Don't dig a tax hole! Earning money via sales commissions changed how I view earning money, and I could never go back to dollars per hour. But earning sales commission as a private contractor means that all the money you make will be in your pocket before the feral or state government pulls out their piece, meaning no paycheck deductions from the state or federal government. Get in the habit of deducting at least 20% of your paycheck and putting it to the side, there's no point in making allot of money and going to jail over it.

When I saw my name attached to a check with six figures,
I knew I was on the right track. This isn't just for me.
I'm not special. I bust my ass, I make connections,
and deliver. This is also for you.

When I saw my name attached to a check with six figures,
I knew I was on the right track. This isn't just for me.
I'm not special. I bust my ass, I make connections,
and deliver. This is also for you.

CHAPTER 4

Tools of the Trade

WHEN I WAS A PHLEBOTOMIST, certain items had to be worn and used every single day during every procedure without fail or discussion:

Face shield- to protect your eyes and mouth from blood.

Lab Coat- to protect your clothes and skin from blood.

Gloves- to protect your hands from blood.

Not having the proper PPE meant the job could not be done, and cannabis sales are no different. You will need specific tools in your belt and on your person to help you stay organized, efficient and orchestrate your daily deals. If you are visiting as many dispensaries as you are supposed to, then there will be a continuous flood of papers, sticky notes, and business cards; without the proper organizational tools, you will start finding papers and business cards in your car cup holder and in the pockets of everything you wear.

I once told an intake manager not to trust a sales rep that shows up without a pen.

How do you sign a deal without a pen?

"Sell me this pen" – Wolf of Wall Street.

If you are a roofer, you better have nails in your pouch and, if you are in weed sales, you had better have a pen! But having a pen is a minimum! Below I have listed the necessary equipment for the sales battlefield.

- Car with ample space and in good working condition- Driving is what you do! Having a reliable car is an absolute must, you will have to drive long distances, and you don't want to be stuck on the side of the road. As you grow in the industry, so will how much product you carry; constantly be assessing if you have outgrown your vehicle.
- Laptop or Tablet with service- You will absolutely need a laptop! But if you get a tablet with your cell phone company, that will be best. The ability to check inventory, send emails, create manifests and take notes on the go is essential.
- Cell phone with good service- Who here likes bad service? How about bad service that costs you money? You will probably drive to some pretty rural areas, so having a good cell phone carrier will give you fewer headaches and frustrations and allow you to communicate with HQ if you must

reach out. I started with Sprint but have been with Verizon for the past three years; you must have service everywhere!

- Cell Phone charging block- Dead cell phones = no communication = No sales. Yes, you can charge in the car, but there will be times when that battery pack will save your sales day; have it on the ready.

- Ability to charge phone FAST in the car- You live in your car and on your phone. Have a good charger/cable- None of that slow charging crap!

- Receipt Book or digital invoice creator- Yes, a paper invoice book will work, but I highly recommend using a digital invoice creator like skynova.com. They have a cheap monthly fee and give you the ability to create Invoices at a moment's notice. Digital invoices are also easier to manage and email to clients. They stay organized by date and company, making any invoice easy to find at any time. I can't even count the number of times my customers have asked me to resend a certain invoice months later.

- Water receptacle- You will be in your car for 3-5 hours minimum a day. If you don't bring water, you won't drink water. YOU ARE MADE OF WATER. BRING WATER.

- Business card organizer- You must stay on top of filing your business cards. File your cards away daily, and you won't find them all over the place, and what's better, you will be able to find the card you are looking for when the time comes.

- Stapler- Clutch! Much better than paper clips for keeping papers together. The more sales you make, the more manifests and invoices you will have floating around.

- Envelopes- Where are you putting your money after you receive it? You will start collecting thousands a day. Seal and Label as follows- Who is the Payee, the Amount, who the money belongs to and the date.

- 6-8 Item organizational folder

- Daily planner- This is an absolute must in sales, and for life in general. Write out your week, every week! Give yourself vision into your week. This will give you a strong confidence boost. Your planner is your weekly map. Fill out the directions, so you get where you want to go. A daily planner allows you to get appointment and follow up information on paper, so you don't have to stress out trying to remember what someone said or what next steps you need to take.

- Laptop bag or backpack- If you can't tell from this list, you will have a lot to keep together and in one place. Whether you prefer a backpack or good size laptop bag, having one of these is necessary.

- Printer- A printer/ scanner combo for home is very crucial. You can forgo one in the beginning and use UPS printing or any other printing places around. But it will simplify your life and save you time in the long run. No more leaving early to have to print documents

Sales Hack: Closing out the day- At the end of every day, take the time to file, turn in, and throw away paperwork. If you don't, your old papers will get mixed in with your new papers, making it frustrating and time-consuming when you try to find the right papers. Start the job with a multi file folder.

Sales Hack: Rock the Fanny Pack: The fanny pack is like your construction tool belt, it will hold your pens, sharpies, keys, mask, air pods, lighter, cell phone. I have found the fanny pack to be essential to my every day, keeps all my tools on me and my pockets empty.

The best $100 investment I've ever made in my life. Invest in yourself and you'll be surprised by what you do for you.

CHAPTER 5

The Prettiest Baby

FLOWER PRODUCERS WILL ALWAYS FEEL as if their flower is the best of the best and deserves top dollar! Convincing them otherwise is usually a pain but necessary. Just as a mother gives all the effort required in carrying her baby for nine months, when that baby comes out, to her, it's the most beautiful baby in the world! Trying to convince her otherwise is practically a death sentence.

Cannabis farmers are no different. They have spent long, arduous hours growing and spent hundreds of thousands of dollars just to get the product to the point of viewing and selling. Trying to convince them that they need to come down on price can be as sensitive as telling a mother her baby just isn't model material!

Knowing how to judge and price flower is a handy and necessary skill. It will allow you to have knowledgeable conversations with growers when discussing what price, they should be around and will allow you to reach for the top price and top shelf in a dispensary with confidence.

In order to get the highest price for your flower, your flower must have 2 of the 3 or all 3 qualities that create the flower trifecta! These three qualities are the selling point of the flower, they sell the weed to the dispensary purchaser and to the dispensary's customers.

The flower trifecta = Look + smell + THC %.

If your flower stands out in all these categories, it has what I call "The Trifecta". Within a dispensary, these aspects of your flower will have the greatest effect on your selling price, bring all three to the table, and you will be able to name your price.

Look

Has the flower been hand trimmed or machine trimmed? Are the nugs dense and shapely or airy and leafy? Is it Frosty white and covered in trichomes, or is the THC barely visible? Does it have seeds or seed pockets? Is it colorful? Answering these visual questions when evaluating your flower will give you a great indication of where your flower stands with its "jar appeal." Jar appeal is the term dispensary managers use when referring to a customer eyeballing flower on the shelf. As Humans, we are instinctually drawn to things that are aesthetically pleasing, and weed is no different.

Terpenes

How's the nose? Does the cannabis flower smell like hay? Is it gassy like gasoline? Does it smell fruity? Does it smell piney? Or like dirt? Did the farm let the flower cure correctly? Does the flower smell like it's supposed to smell for the genetics that are being represented? I have received many replies to messages from intake managers asking, "How's the nose?" after propositioning them via text or email with a strain for sale. When it comes to purchasing flower in a dispensary, I always tell customers to use their third eye when shopping; your third eye is your nose! A flower with a strong nose will take your flower close to the sales finish line. If the aroma is strong, it will grab the intake manager by the nose and make their eyes light up. If you are going to take selling weed seriously, then you must learn where and what the smell of your weed is attributed to. The smell that comes from weed is determined by the specific terpenes that are expressed through the genetics of the plant. Like humans having a different funk, each strain is different and produces different terpenes/ smells. Know your scents, know your terpenes. There are more than 20,000 known terpenes in the world, and cannabis produces over 100 of these terpenes.

Terpenes have a lot more to do with your high than you might currently know, and it will be up to you to discover that beautiful science. If you can convey that knowledge in a meeting with the purchasing manager, you will be steps closer to the sale than someone who knows nothing of the terpenes their product produces.

THC%

This is the last leg of the race for pricing flower, and, unfortunately, it will make or break your price. THC percentage is the holy grail for a flower within a dispensary. It immediately adds to or takes away from the value of a flower. Though I and anyone who understands the science behind cannabis do not agree with this, the consumers that come in to buy weed believe that the higher the THC percentage attached to the flower, the higher you will get/ feel. Due to this misbelief, intake managers use THC % to help dictate what price they will pay and what tier your flower will make it on. Due to a lack of consistency throughout different laboratories and their processes, it is impossible to say what THC percentage a flower might have even after testing it. I have witnessed flower covered in trichomes come back with THC% around 16 and have seen flower with no visible THC come back with THC testing in the 28-29%. It is unfortunate, but the higher the THC percentage given to you by the lab, the higher price you will get for your flower.

Sales Hack: **Roll the bag-** You want the intake manager to have the best interactive experience with your flower when you are in front of them. If your flower is in a turkey bag or any type of bag you can roll up, do so. Roll the bag down so that the nugs are poking over the top of the bag, this will allow them to get their eyes and nose as close to the flower as possible. Once the bag is rolled back, and the purchaser is inspecting your flower closely, I like to create an image in their mind with the following line: "Can you see your customers smelling/ looking at a jar of that? That's an instant purchase". Essentially, you want to provide/ help the intake manager have the same experience with the flower as their customer. If they can visualize their customer seeing, smelling, and being excited about your weed, then you are one step closer to the sale.

Sales Hack: Start High- If you have been given a floor price that the flower can't go under, be sure to start a little higher with your asking price. I call this building in your wiggle room. Your purchaser will certainly say they would be interested if the price was lower, so if you start with $100 over the floor price, this will give you wiggle room to come down in price without going below the floor price.

I love visiting grow sites

CHAPTER 6

Dress the Part

WOULD YOU SHOW UP TO a job interview with toothpaste stains on your shirt, pants falling off your ass, and grungy shoes? Then don't go meeting purchasing managers for the first time looking that way either. Meeting an owner or purchasing manager for the first time should be viewed as a job interview because that's exactly what it is!

This industry may be full of stoners, but we are all human and make judgments based on first impressions, just like everyone else. Show up looking like a mess or like you just rolled out of bed, and they will assume that doing business with you will be the same. Half put together, missing items they ordered and having to chase you down for sales paperwork. You want your first meeting to give them the impression and belief that doing business with you will make their life easier, that out of all the other vendors that come to sell them cannabis products, you are the one that will simplify their purchasing life. This will all be assumed by how you present yourself and how well you connect with them in your first meeting.

Once I met with a realtor to check out a prospective property, he pulled up in a beautiful blue Mercedes Benz; whether he was good at selling properties or not, just from seeing him pull up made me very confident about working with him. I am not saying that your attire defines you or that you must always have to wear your Sunday best, but make sure that your personal style reflects your personality and your work ethic and portrays serious you take what you do. In cannabis sales, there is no such thing as being overdressed, but you can be underdressed.

I work with a dispensary in Oregon that doesn't even call me by my name anymore. In one of our first meetings, I wore an Italian scarf that matched my loafers and have worn loafers every time I have done business with them. They now call me loafers! They were thrown off that a cannabis sales rep dresses the way I do and even thought it a little funny, but now they get it. This is Benjamin. This is his style- it is unique- it matches his outgoing personality, he is sharp, on point, and that's how working with him is as well.

Sales Hack: Always show up in clothes that speak to who you are. Your clothes are an extension of your personality!! You want Intake managers to feel how comfortable and confident you are. Your clothes and energy should make them feel as if they know you; you are the homie, and you are always like this, this is how you dress, this is who you are! The more comfortable they are around you, the more they will want you around- remember there are many people selling a very similar product- People buy from people they trust and know! Don't sell product. Sell yourself.

Sales Hack: Sheep in wolves' clothes: When you are in the industry long enough you will build some great relationships with a variety of shops, during this time period many of them will get you their own company swag, many will hook you up with beanies, hoodies, T shirts that have their company logo or name on them. Be careful wearing other dispensary clothing out on your sales days, you never know the history or beef between dispensaries. I know several dispensaries that despise each other and would be completely turned off/ hurt my relationship if they knew I was repping/ came in to do sales wearing their enemies clothing. Sometimes there is bad blood from issues between owners, or maybe the one dispensary purchased a billboard that is directly next to or above a rivalling dispensary, or sometimes shops copycat other shops sales tactics and the word gets out. I tend to leave dispensary gear that I receive for the weekends or camping, you don't want to find out about bad blood by coming by to do sales in the enemy's clothing and then get an earful on why that other shop can eat shit and die! The beef be that bad! I do however wear any gear I get from farms, or other companies that produce cannabis products for the industry. Gear from these companies is much more acceptable and allot less likely to be representing the "enemy" in other dispensaries eyes.

CHAPTER 7

Vendor Day Magic

IF YOU ARE UNDER THE impression that your sole job is to sell products to dispensaries, you are wrong. Selling products into a shop is only half the battle, once your product makes it on the shelf the next hurdle is making sure your product gets sold to the consumer, otherwise it will sit on the dispensary shelf selling at a snail's pace and you won't get a reorder; or worse you will lose your shelf space to another product that does. Well, that's the budtenders job you might say, and you would be right and wrong at the same time. Think back to your meeting with the purchaser, when you were selling them on the reason they should put your product on the shelf, what were the things you said? What did you say that really drove the point home and convinced them to purchase your product? Does the budtender know this information? What is the budtender even telling the customers about your product? What the budtender is saying, or not saying can be preventing your product from being sold in the dispensary. With how many products occupy

39

the dispensary shelves in a dispensary, its hard for consumers to notice when something new arrives, this is where your battle continues. Thankfully there is a way for you to sell your product within the dispensary, and also grow your value and relationship with the dispensary at the same time.

Vendor days
These events are the **KEY** to substantial and sustained relationship development between you and your dispensary accounts, vendor days are where you talk the talk and walk the walk.

What the hell is a vendor day?
This is a day in which you have previously arranged a time and day to show up to that dispensary and sell your product within the shop, your company should arm you with a table, table skirt, company swag, product knowledge pamphlets or posters, and usually a pre discussed discount % or promotion that is agreed upon between the dispensary and your company (the discount is usually split between the two companies).

There are ways to ensure your vendor day is a success, and there are ways of doing nothing that will ensure your vendor day was just a waste of your time. Remember, time is your most valuable asset, avoid wasting it at all costs. Just as if any event is to be successful, people must know and be aware that its even happening. The first key to throwing a successful vendor day is getting the word out at least two weeks ahead of the event. There should be physical advertisements around the shop and ads on your company's social media as well as the dispensaries social media, the advertisement should state your company name, product, the promotion being run, whether the promotion is for the whole day or only while you are present at the dispensary, and the date and time period in which you will be on site; vendor days are usually held between three and four hours. The second key to a successful vendor day is probably my favorite part, engaging with the customers that walk in the dispensary. The point of even being there is to sell the product to the dispensary customers, if you only stand quietly behind your table, you will not sell as much as you could if you walked around the shop and talked to the customers. Whenever I work a vendor day, I approach each customer as soon as they walk in the door, I greet them with a smile and a welcome in, let them know who I am, the product I am representing, and the promotion being run. It really is that simple, there are a limited number of cannabis product the customer can come in for, so you have a one out of five chance that they came in looking for a cannabis product in your lane. If they aren't interested or don't partake in your type of product then you tell them to have a great day and talk to the next customer, you are not there to force anyone to purchase from you, but with the right attitude and a good promotion, you are likely to rack up sales for the shop; or better yet sell all your product off the shelf and show the dispensary the need for a re order. It is possible and should be your personal goal to sell as much of your product as you can when doing a vendor day, I have thrown vendor events where I completely sold all the units the dispensary had on hand and before I was packed up for the day the dispensary manager came out and asked for another order and if it could be delivered the next day. You have more control over your sales than just making sure they get on the shelves of the dispensaries, force dispensaries to reorder by showing them your product is what their customers want; bottom line is they will purchase what their customers want.

Successful vendor days move product, successful vendor days show you genuinely care for how your product does within a dispensary, successful vendor days will show budtenders how to sell your product. After hearing your approach and methods of selling your product for three to four hours, budtenders will begin to model your lingo and story to sell the product when you are not there, next thing you know your product is moving off the shelves at the same rate as when you are there, this is the mark of a successful vendor day.

Sales Hack: Swag trade- There are a couple strategies I have used in order to guarantee good sales numbers while running a vendor day. If your company provides you with awesome swag- Shirts, Hoodies, water bottles, fitted hats, beanies, leverage the swag for purchases. As you are telling the customer about the limited time discount, offer them something off your table in return for the purchase. From their POV they are receiving a discounted cannabis product and getting something for free, this works for almost all customers. The better your company's swag, logo, and product are, the easier it is to persuade customers to trade a purchase for your company swag.

Sales Hack- Teachable moment: Whenever you are in the dispensary running a vendor day, be sure the bud tenders learn some of the things you are saying to the customers about your product. This way, when you leave, they will be able to sell your product, the biggest reason for slow sales in a dispensary is the budtenders just don't know what to say or how to sell your product. Make sure you get all the best uses out of your vendor day, move units of what you sold to the shop and teach the budtenders how to sell your product.

Our first vendor day event, representing
our brand: Lifted Lifestyle

CHAPTER 8

Car Insurance

YOUR JOB IS 80% DRIVING. To have or not to have insurance is not the question. **You must have car insurance**! You will be in the morning traffic, the afternoon traffic, and driving during the day with the elderly. Having your vehicle protected should not be an expense you skimp on. Without a vehicle, you can't bounce from dispensary to dispensary, and you might as well not be a sales rep. An old sales associate of mine used a bicycle for the first quarter of his sales career, he would wear a large duffle as a backpack and stuff it with his product for sale. After a few months of this he realized this was not a sustainable option, he then moved up to a moped, then to a truck. If you were to ask him, I'm sure he will advise you against anything but a motorized vehicle with four doors. But his willingness to make sales happen from his bicycle, guaranteed that he would stay in the cannabis sales game and do well once he located a vehicle.

Insurance companies want to get paid just like you,

at all costs; and will defend their right to not pay for your vehicle claim if you are caught without the right vehicle coverage. There is a specific type of insurance you must have if you are using your vehicle for operations other than transportation. Commercial vehicle insurance is required if the following definition defines how, you are using your vehicle.

1. If you are collecting money for work, service, or product delivery. Cannabis sales require that you do both several times a day, so you are required to have this specific insurance.

When you are working for Uber, Lyft, Postmates, or any service where you receive payment for a service, you must have commercial insurance coverage on your vehicle; and cannabis sales are no different. In the insurance world, they surmise that you are in your vehicle more than average and you use your vehicle for getting money, so yes, they will charge you more. You can certainly get away with only having normal everyday car insurance coverage for your vehicle, but if you are ever in a fender bender while enroute to a dispensary or farm, you better be sure to keep the true nature of your activity close to the chest.

I am not telling you what to do, nor am I advocating for insurance fraud, but to be involved in a car accident on the job and only have regular car insurance coverage could leave you footing the vehicle repair bill if your words implicate you to be using your vehicle in a way that is not covered by your insurance. If you don't have commercial insurance coverage on your vehicle it would behoove you to tread lightly around the nature of your being at that place in time. Being on the way to the grocery store, going home from a friend's house, heading to a dentist appointment, do not constitute the requirement of commercial insurance. If you are found to be working through your vehicle without the proper vehicle insurance coverage, they could find you operating outside the terms of your insurance contract and not cover any of the damages.

With driving being the foundation of this position, I **highly** recommend getting commercial insurance coverage when you can afford it. It is certainly a steeper cost per month but will keep you on the road making the kind of money that makes your insurance payment look like peanuts.

Sales Hack: Watch that led foot! I say this, but it is hard even for me. As sales reps, we are always on the go, and that can lead to speeding from one place to another. Be a master of time management so that you can keep a relaxed mind and the need to speed to a minimum. Speeding tickets will raise your insurance premiums, and too many tickets can get your license suspended in a short time frame. You need insurance and a license to be a sales rep, manage your time well, so you don't talk yourself into speeding.

Sales Hack: Leave the road rage in the cage. Being behind the wheel all day means you will have to learn the art of self-control and learn to control your temper behind the wheel. Aggressive and angry energy in the car is guaranteed to transfer into your sales appointments and will not conjure the vibe that people want to be around. Can you imagine getting road rage every time you drive? Now multiply those times fifty and you're basically pissed off all day. When I started as a sales rep, I believed road rage was just a thing that happened and was a normal mode to transform into every time I got behind the wheel. It's not. I read a book that explained the reason it's so easy to get road rage, in short, your brain gets addicted to the chemicals that are released when you get angry. When the brain wants the chemicals and realizes that road rage is the vehicle to release those chemicals, you've now got a setup of getting angry behind the wheel. Pro longed road rage behavior makes your body accustomed to the release of certain chemicals; therefore, your brain starts looking for situations that will produce those chemicals, and when you are walking towards the car the brain gets ready to get what it wants. It's you vs. you out on the road. Either get better or stay pissed off. Enter the car with the thought that you will practice kindness with the drivers you encounter on the road, let people go first, allow people to pass you if they are riding you, take nothing personally. All of this is easier said than done, but you will certainly have time to practice with all the time you are in the car.

CHAPTER 9

You gotta Be Hungry for Sales all Day, Every day!

Monday is better than Friday.
Change my mind.

YOU LIKE GETTING PAID, RIGHT? Picture this! From Friday through Sunday the dispensary sells, sells, sells, and purchases zero product all weekend. Come Monday the purchaser or owner is back at work and looking to fill any gaps in inventory replacing any products they ran through over the weekend. Every Monday means dispensary wallets are open, and purchasers are looking to spend money! Tell me a day more exciting than that. Can you feel the excitement for Monday? Can you feel motivation building from your thoughts whirling around the perceived possibility of increased sales? Land any sales position, and you will instantly feel this motivation for Monday. Sales opportunities will come throughout the week, but Mondays are guaranteed traction! Hit enough dispensaries on a Monday, and you will put numbers on the board and money in your pocket.

Everyone thinks they want to sell weed until they start selling weed. Your car will become your new home. You will eat there, sleep there, lose your mind in traffic and find your peace there. You will have to put up with all of this and more, and some days not even record a sale, and yet you must wake up the following day with optimism and excitement for more! Yes, generating sales is the ultimate win, but in the very beginning, you may see infrequent sales or not generate a lot of income. Your small victories must mean a lot to you. They must inspire you to wake up another day and go get your money! Selling weed is not for the faint of heart or people with trouble being self-motivated. You must be motivated by the sales deals you come up with using your sales imagination. You create the deal, you create the excitement, you create the motivation! One of the ultimate keys to selling cannabis products is being and staying highly self-motivated. You must be motivated to action by everything you see, think, and do. You can even create motivating sales ideas through your losses if you perceive them correctly, losses in sales indicate you were a decision, idea, or move away from landing the sale: will you pivot and try again? It is up to you to find motivation in the perceived opportunities within your day-to-day sales activities; you must have vision and imagination; you must be able to see the sale!!

I view every single interaction in my sales day as a W!

You woke up and put pants on? WIN! You didn't make any sales today but got a bunch of sales information on your dispensaries? WIN! You go into a dispensary without an appointment, and they tell you to get the fuck out? WIN!

How? you ask. You had the guts to walk in the dispensary and try, right? Then that is a win. All experience gained is a WIN! You will always learn more from your losses than you will from your wins. Your wins can lead you to believe you crushed it, when in reality, you barely pulled it off. Triumph over your losses, knowing you will gain knowledge, skill, and wisdom along the way, creating a highly trained sales professional.

One day you will be able to sell ice to an Eskimo.

3/26/20- Covid-19 is in full swing, and everyone working in the cannabis industry has been deemed essential and permitted to continue working. The roads are eerily empty as most people are inside their homes and only come out to buy water, toilet paper, and weed. I'm cruising a road I often travel when I notice a dispensary that I've never seen before. "What the hell?" I exclaim. I immediately take the next left, circle back around, and park across the street. I jump out of my vehicle and scurry over to wait in the line that has formed outside (due to social distancing, dispensaries were allowing no more than two people inside at a time). After gaining entry, I interrogate the budtenders to extract as much information as possible. After getting all useful information out of the frontline, make a move to see if the purchaser is available, speaking with new shops is my favorite, after being seasoned in sales you can smell when a purchaser is new to the game; they will usually cough up quite a bit of great info. "Hello, my name is Benjamin, and I have questions!" When did you open? Are you vertically integrated? Are there any Cannabis products or price points you are having difficulty locating? Do you guys have more than one shop? etc. *"Insert rapport and relationship building here. Welcome to the neighborhood!"*

No sale was recorded on this day, but I came out of my meeting motivated for the next dispensary, and I am over the top excited about the future with this shop! I just met a new potential buying customer and gathered valuable intel that will allow me to bring them the exact products they are hunting for. My efforts have made a sale much more probable on my next visit, and I can already imagine how the next meeting will go. I am fueled by the excitement of the next time I stop by. Allow yourself to get excited!

As you may have started to gather, your imagination and excitement are tied together. The more imagination you use to visualize deals, the more excitement you will generate about landing them. Thoughts that generate excitement around landing deals will build an internal motivation to visit more dispensaries. By this, you will naturally attract your sales through thought and action.

Your excitement and imagination are the fuel to your motivation.

Driving by a blank building with a sign that says "Dispensary coming soon" can be one of the most exciting things. You must learn to view empty dispensaries as a blank canvas. When I come across a brand-new dispensary that isn't even open yet, my imagination and excitement go through the roof! I always stop and put my card in the door, then case the joint by looking around the premises to see if the owners are around; being the first vendor the owners come across has its perks. If you are the early bird when it comes to meeting the owners/ product purchasers of a new dispensary, you can fill a shop with every line of product you sell.

Look at every new shop as a birthday present you are excited to unwrap. Let that excitement stir your imagination! The monetary possibilities within can be limitless, be motivated by every interaction!

Sales HACK: Trust your gut. If you ever drive by a dispensary and feel like you should just stop in, do it. Your gut is telling you for a reason. I have attained numerous sales from pulling over and popping into a random dispensary I was driving by. All from a gut feeling.

SALES HACK: Use your drive time to grow. I love music as much as anyone who has the talent to play a musical instrument. But we spend enough time in the car to learn and build new habits and ways of thinking. Instead of listening to music all day, use some of your drive time to listen to motivational podcasts, books on finance, personal growth, or on anything else you want to learn.

CHAPTER 10

Line Up Your Ducks!

THERE IS A WONDERFUL LEVEL of ease and professionalism that comes with working with a person that is organized and timely, and there is a headache and displeasure that comes with a person who isn't. Intake managers want to work with sales reps that make their lives easier. They want to work with sales reps they don't have to chase for pertinent information regarding a sale. Every sale has critical information that must be provided to the dispensary before they can put the product on the sales floor. If you make sure they don't have to bug you for the following information, you will be doing much to ensure that they call you for repeat business.

Invoice- Make sure you either have this on your person when dropping off the product or have emailed it to the purchaser before your arrival. At the dispensary level, the invoice serves many purposes. Not only is it how a dispensary tracks its spending, but it is also the dispensary's pricing guide. Dispensaries purchase products that fall into specific price categories that match the quality at a given price point, without an invoice, they would have to guess what they paid for your product; either pricing it too high in which the product doesn't sell, or too low where they are losing money. They will bug you until they get this piece of information, be on top of your game and give it to them before they ask for it.

COA- Also known as the Certificate of Analysis or, as I call it, the labs. This paperwork provides the dispensary with the scientific laboratory tests run on cannabis products to ensure they are safe for human consumption. Every state will require different analytical tests to be run on the cannabis products provided in the industry, and each type of product will have its own required tests (Flower, Extracts, Edibles, Cartridges). They test these products for mold, pesticides, additives, heavy metals, THC levels, other cannabinoid content, Terpene content, and many other compounds. The product cannot be put out on the sales floor until they receive the labs!! No store will take the risk of possibly putting out untested products, so have the COA readily available.

Manifest- This is the legal transfer paperwork that shows what is being transferred, how much is being transferred, both company names and locations the product is being transferred between, who the driver is, and their estimated arrival time. Hands down, this is the most vital piece of paperwork in a sale. If something is off or wrong on this paperwork, it could put the whole sale off. This document will not be emailed ahead of time but is something you must have on your person any time you have weed products. This piece of paper doubles as your get out of jail free card if you are ever stopped and questioned by the police. Between your sale and your freedom, it would behoove you to ensure this paperwork's accuracy before you drive off with any weed products.

In the beginning of my sales career, I drove to a dispensary that was 4 hours away only to arrive and find out that the items manifested were incorrect. The person who prepared my manifest looked at the wrong sales order and sent me with the wrong product. But! This error was completely my fault, this position is all about personal responsibility. I left the warehouse without checking over MY manifest paperwork. Knowing the dispensary was so far away, I should have matched the invoice, product and manifest before leaving the building. 8hrs of driving, no sale. Needless to say, this has never happened to me again. The worst thing for a sales rep is wasted time. Always double-check your paperwork.

Sales Hack: Double-check- Whether you created your manifest, and especially if you didn't, be sure to go over the manifest line by line before you take off for delivery. Make sure you check over all TAG numbers, making sure the tags on the items you are delivering match the product printed on the manifest (these are easy to

mistype and can bring up an entirely different product.) Read over the item names of what is being shipped and the amounts being shipped. If a dispensary has multiple shops, ensure you have been manifested to the correct location.

Sales Hack: Take Control- Being able to create your invoice on the fly is essential! If a dispensary pays you COD, they will want an invoice before you leave. Save yourself time from standing around waiting by having your own invoice creator, either the classic paper invoice book (I used this the first two years) or use a digital service- I personally use Aynax.com- $25/month- allows you to create digital invoices you can email and alphabetically saved online.

Ever outgrow a safe? In this industry you will!

CHAPTER 11

Where the Cash At!

*"Cash rules everything around me, C.R.E.A.M get
the money; dolla bill y'all"*
– Wu-Tang Clan

WITH CASH COMES GREAT POWER, and with great power comes
great responsibility!

Businesses are going to give you their explicit trust.
Not only will you be trusted by the company that employs
you, to bring their money back, but also by the dispensaries handing you their payments to clear their debt. Trust
takes quite some time to build and only a fraction of the
time to destroy. Once the trust is broken, it's never quite
the same even if corrected.

Protect their trust in you at all costs!

Always, Always, Always!!! count all the money handed to
you by anyone! Due to a lack of banking, this industry

is very cash-heavy; dispensaries receive a lot of cash, so that's how they like to pay.

Have you ever held $10,000, $20,000 dollars? Well, you're about to handle that much and a lot more!

Most dispensaries have a cash counter, and depending on how much you are picking up, you may need to ask to use it ($10,000 in twenty-dollar denominations can take a while to count by hand). When picking up payments, make sure you recount the stacks handed to you while in front of them. I have come to notice that most dispensaries want you to recount the money they hand you, that way you both can confirm that there are no discrepancies in the payment pickup. If anyone ever says to me that "I don't need to count the money", a red flag immediately goes off in my head! That is when I would reply with, "I would rather double-check". If they reply with "What you don't trust me?" (2ND Red Flag) Then I let them know that we are humans and humans make mistakes.

As you grow in sales, so will the amount of money you pick up and the amount you have on hand at one time. You need to have systems and procedures in place that you follow unconditionally every time you finish a transaction. Not having a system means you will have payments in random places and set yourself up to lose one. Like I did.

In my second year of sales, I had a repeat sale with one of my most consistent shops- they have a standing order with me to deliver two pounds of flower every week on Saturday morning, amounting to $1800, and they pay COD. This dispensary and I have a trust that some people don't even have with their family members. I don't have to ask if they want an order or what flower they want to bring in; I just bring what I know they like, and they pay me. This had been a repeat order every Saturday for over a year.

To say the least, they trust me!

On a particularly normal Saturday, I had dropped off the two lbs of flower, collected the money, and headed out for brunch with some friends. What a beautiful way to start the weekend, $180 in commission for less than 30 minutes of work. I had the $1800 rubber-banded up and hanging out in my shorts pocket- **WRONG!** A couple of mimosas in, and I was thinking nothing about that $1800 just hanging out in my pocket. As you can guess, the $1800 fell out of my pocket at some point, and I didn't even notice until the end of the day. Talk about turning a great day into a miserable one.

In this situation, you have two options. Option 1. Burn multiple bridges- The bridge with the dispensary and the bridge with the farmer/ company you are selling for, or Option 2. Fix the situation from your side, and you replace the money! Truth of the matter, there is only one option. **Never burn bridges**. It's not worth it. If you cause the mistake, do everything to recompense what you must. I ended up replacing the money with money I had been saving and chalked it up to a lesson learned. I was pissed off at myself for weeks, and after reading this, if you make the same error in judgment; you should also be highly pissed off at yourself also! Let the anger provoke change in your cash handling procedures to create a solid process that you stick to. You will probably be hurting financially for a few weeks, but with pain comes growth, it is now two years later, and I have lost 0 payments since.

SALES HACK: Always Count the cash!

Step 1. Confirm all funds being picked up every time! Do not get lazy or comfortable- People make mistakes counting money all the time- and that will be a mistake that comes out of your pocket. Even if it's a lot of money and must be run through a money counter or counted by hand. Verify Verify Verify!

Step 2. After collecting the funds, have a place that the money goes into every time and ensure that you follow the same process every time.

Sales Hack: Cash envelope organization- I purchase boxes of envelopes so that after every sale, I immediately place the money in an envelope. I label the envelope with how much is inside, the name of the shop the money is from, and the name of the farm or company the sale is for; then I place the envelope into my money bag, zip the bag closed, and placed in a storing place. I do this immediately after picking up any funds EVERY TIME.

Companies will implicitly trust you. Never break or lose the trust of anyone in the industry. If word gets out, you are involved in bad business your money well will dry up.

Always buckle up for safety. I had to deposit this through the outside window at the bank. Due to Covid, they weren't letting people come into the bank. I filled the cash tray about 5 times to get this transaction done.

What's the point of having money if you can't play with it! This is $700,000 piled on my best friend in Colorado. He helped get us to the bank and made sure we were safe.

CHAPTER 12

Emails, Calls, In person visits

AT THIS POINT, YOU SHOULD have already visually digested that being in the dispensary face to face with the purchaser is one of the most important and consistent things **YOU MUST** be doing. I can't stress it enough. Please understand that this action or lack of can make or break your weed sales career. Every action you take should put you in front of the purchaser. This is the only person a sale can be made with. Though being in front of the purchaser is one of the most critical elements of selling cannabis products, truth be told, just walking into dispensaries isn't the guaranteed way to get in front of them every time. What if you walk in and they are busy? What if the last five times you have stopped in without an appointment, they have been "busy"?

In this chapter, I want to discuss two subtle forms of contact that can increase the likelihood of you getting in front of the purchaser. Emails and Phone Calls- the smarter and not harder way to nail down a guaranteed appointment, but also certainly how you will be screened and ignored, so make sure you still get your face in the dispensary.

Emails- You know how you scan over the emails in your generic email, the email address that you give out to businesses, and people you don't want to contact you? Well, that's how intake managers parous their email inbox, and honestly, I can't blame them. If you can imagine, vendor emails are like darts, and the purchasing manager's email address is a dart board; and their weekly spending limit appears as the bullseye. Now imagine so many darts flying at the dartboard that the sky turns to black and blocks out the sun; that's the email volume purchasers deal with. Unless you have spoken with the purchaser directly and you confirm with them to be looking for your menu in their email, don't take it personally when you send ten emails and hear nothing back.

So how do you get your email to catch their eye?

Put the meat and potatoes of your email in the subject line. Give them no choice but to be curious about opening your email. I have written things like "Bulk buy*** 10lbs @ 1,000/lb)", or "$400 lbs available!!", in as the subject. If they even have the slightest curiosity, they will open your email.

Phone calls- This is something you can do at the beginning of your sales day to lock in appointments for that day. If you start the day with a list of shops you will visit, I suggest calling them early before the shop purchaser gets too busy. When you call a dispensary, you always have the off chance that the person you are looking for (the purchaser) answers the phone, or they are not too busy and can accept your call. If you are lucky, they will give you a moment of their time over the phone, this is your opportunity to hook them with your deal; so, make it short and to the point. The object here is to set a time for them to agree to have an appointment with you, not build rapport.

Texting- The more you visit a shop and build your relationship with the purchaser, the higher probability of them giving you their personal cell number; this is good, and this is also a trap. YES, getting the personal number of the purchaser is a great step in the building of your relationship; it proves that you have earned their trust and they are happy with what you bring to the table, but it also means that instead of calling the shop to set up an appointment or just stopping in; you will be tempted to only text and see if they need anything or if you may stop in for a quick visit. Though this is a more direct route of communication, it will allow you to be ghosted or left on read more often.

How many texts do you have in your phone inbox right now that you read quickly when you received them, and told yourself that you would reply shortly, but still haven't?

Without a reply, you will feel as if they are ignoring you, or perhaps they just don't want you to come in. You check the text thread, and they haven't replied in five messages (sent on different days, don't badger). Now what? Should you never go in again? Silence is an answer, right?

Negative!

This leads us back to the beginning of this sales guide. If the replies stop, you stop texting and get your face in the shop. Keep in mind that purchasers are busy on their personal phone, the company phone, their email, and in-person visits. You must learn the balance of communication with purchasers and afford them leeway to forget. You can be their memory by gauging the type of communication needed, according to the communication they are giving you. By this I suggest that if they aren't replying to text and email, it's time to just stop by... cough cough, which you should ALWAYS be doing anyway.

SALES Hack: Early Bird gets noticed- If you start your sales week on Monday, then you are behind. Send your emails about your upcoming weekly deals/ menu on Sunday afternoon. Most purchasers are looking over shop inventory and figuring out what is needed for their shop; now imagine your email popping up right in the middle of this.

Most sales reps wait until Monday to email the purchaser of a dispensary! Don't let your email get lost in the hordes of emails flooding their Inbox- Here is a

list of your Monday morning email competition- Office Supplies, Insurance Companies, coffee companies, water jug companies, security companies, snack companies, Cannabis software companies, oh yea and don't forget your actual competition- extract makers, cartridge makers, flower producers, edible makers, wholesalers.

SALES HACK: Don't be a class 5 clinger: If a purchaser gives you their personal number, don't make them wish they hadn't. There is a fine line between following up, informing, and being a human gnat. If you are too pushy via text, you can be assured that they will stop replying and buying from you.

CHAPTER 13

Don't sell weed

IN THE RECREATIONAL MARKET, THERE is good weed and great
weed around every corner, so going into a dispensary and
trying to gas up your weed by talking about "how organic
it is" and how "amazing your farms growing techniques
are" will help little to none. Sure, all that back story helps
them paint a picture of the grow, but truth be told, weed
sells itself! The hand-crafted artisanal shape of the nugs
and the sweet smell of dank do all the talking. Therefore,
I don't sell weed.

I sell myself.

Anyone who has ever purchased weed in the black
market can relate to the following scenario- Your connect
is customarily 2 hours late, and upon arrival, he wants to
explain the many reasons he is late. After a ten-minute
synopsis of how his life has been, he gets down to business and hands you a baggie of heavenly scented chronic
and tells you the price. While staring at the nugs and listening to the price, what are the two things that would

sell you on that bag at that price? Look + smell divided by price will tell you if you think the price is fair or if you are going to ask for a discount.

Now transport that same transaction into the dispensary purchaser's office and insert any cannabis product that can be sold in a dispensary; if you have an appointment, don't be two hours late. It will take the purchaser no time at all to scan over your cannabis product and determine if the quality presented in your product matches the current market price for something of similar quality. Without the evolution of your relationship, the entire interaction between you and the purchaser would be over in five minutes, and there would be zero difference between you and the next person with a "great cannabis product".

Though I have approached the above sales meeting from a flower selling perspective, it does not change the fact you should be selling yourself and not your product. No matter what cannabis product you are selling, you will need to focus more on building rapport than selling your product. Whether you are selling cartridges, extracts, edibles, or joints, they will want samples at the end of your presentation to ensure the taste and high associated with your product will be something their customers would enjoy. The purchaser must believe the quality and price you are selling your products will have a chance at competing on their shelves with the similar products.

Imagine if you will, an intake manager stuck in a dispensary behind four walls for eight hours a day dealing with customer issues, employee callouts, and being responsible for purchasing all the weed products for the shop. The intake managers are desperate for a distraction and desperate for outside interaction. Make sure you provide the distraction they are looking for by delivering your enthused energy and personality. Don't sell weed. Sell yourself by connecting with them. If you deliver the energy, you deliver the product!

Every interaction you have with a purchaser is a moment to build rapport. Look for and take advantage of all moments to sprinkle in some of your knowledge and personality, obviously none of that fake shit- Don't force it! Be genuine! You are always delivering more than weed, and you are never just simply dropping off samples. You are there delivering a smile, you are delivering energy, you are delivering a laugh; in essence, you are delivering the reason they do business with you. You must bring the atmosphere and the positive energy to them.

When you walk into the dispensary, you will have to inform the bud tender or front desk person that you are a vendor. At that time, they will either give you an email for contacting the purchaser or ask you to wait a minute as they go see if the intake manager will give you the time of day. If you are asked to wait for a chance meeting with the purchaser, use that waiting period wisely by viewing and noticing what product brands are on the shelves and interacting with budtenders; ask questions about the dispensaries products while being helpful and dropping information when appropriate. If there is only one budtender, **NEVER** continue to talk with a budtender when a customer needs help or walks into the shop. Always take a step back and insist that the budtender help them. I believe the dispensary customer takes precedence over information gathering, and to continue to gather intel would be terrible customer service on your end and the budtenders. By doing this, you will convey to anyone watching how much you care about the dispensary's customers and their sales.

A few chapters earlier, I mentioned a dispensary I was able to set up a consistent every Saturday delivery with. I attribute the beginning strength of that relationship to a sales call I received from them late in the day on a Friday. In this instance, the dispensary purchaser for this shop had called me late and informed me that his normal flower drop that he depends on to hold the dispensary over for the weekend was a no show, and he was in desperate need of a flower drop before Saturday. I agreed to bring some flower by and popped in for the guaranteed sale, but when I arrived at the dispensary, they had a line of customers out the door, and the purchasing manager was at the main counter helping bud tend. When I walked in, the purchaser and I linked eyes. He gave me a look of "I'm sorry, but I need to help get this line down," and I waved him off to keep helping the customers and took a seat in the lobby. One hour later, the line was the same length but with different faces. Instead of having a bad attitude or walking out, I used this time to send some emails and interact with customers to lighten how busy they were. Another half-hour passes, and the line has finally made its way back inside the shop, and his two bud tenders have gained control of the situation. Feeling confident that the major rush of the night is over, he waves to me to come back to the office to present the flower I brought for him.

When the opportunity arises, show that you care about their business. In this situation, I showed my care by showing up in the clutch and being patient, ensuring that the customers were taken care of before myself. Little did I know that caring about the dispensary's needs and sales would earn me guaranteed sales for two years.

When you finally get to the back office, your engagement with the intake manager should be some form of "How are you doing today?" or a recall from something personal in a previous meeting. Laugh, make good eye contact, be encouraging, listen to hear, not to reply. Truly care about how they are doing and have a conversation about it, ask for details and offer solutions if you can; sometimes we are therapists and meant to just lend an ear. In the above scenario, the intake manager had a lot to say about some of his budtenders calling out and how his regular flower drop didn't show up, and how that combination had him stressed him all the way out. He explained that me showing up was clutch and meant he would have full jars for the weekend and could take Saturday off.

Sell yourself.

Purchasers are busy people and you meeting won't usually be longer than 20-30 minutes, after you present your product, you are near the end of the sales meeting. They will either say yes or no, you may negotiate price, then you will both decide how to take care of the payment, whether COD or terms. You will prepare the manifest and invoice, and the transaction is complete. I can't stress enough to make sure you are delivering positive energy, a smile or a laugh, you must always be delivering something aside from your cannabis product. You are not a car salesman. If you come in ad are just sales, sales, sales, you won't be any fun to work with. You aren't a vending machine, so don't act like one. Dispense something their money can't buy, and they will always look forward to buying from you.

Sales Hack: Getting Hype in the whip- This may sound crazy, and you may feel crazy when doing it- But it's an undeniable way to create a ball of energy within you that you will have no option but to exude when you walk into a dispensary- While you are in your car (Not in the dispensary parking lot, you will be on camera), SCREAM at the top of your lungs!!! SCREAM YAAAAAHHOOOOOOO! Or FUCK YESS LET'S GET IT!! or whatever your battle cry may be. Tell yourself out loud how much you are about to crush your next meeting; how proud of yourself you are!!! Yell your favorite positive affirmations as loud as you can. Singing your favorite feel-good songs emphatically also works well. Do whatever gets your blood pumping full of positive energy. Do this and you will walk into your meeting radiating positive energy, remember

that energy is and can be transferred and you are a creator of energy.

Sales Hack: Want to be indispensable to a dispensary? Show them value and give them more than just the product you sell. Show them a better way to do a process, help them with a community project, offer to come in and have a vendor day. Learn or notice a problem they are having and help them fix it!! Dispensaries, in essence, are a lot alike but can also be very different depending on location and the owners' priorities. Chances are you will learn new things about dispensaries from visiting a variety of them, and soon will be able to teach these systems/ processes from your other dispensaries and employ them to another dispensaries problem. Be their problem solver, and they will fight to keep you around.

Was blessed to meet the one and only Redman, he popped up at my friend's dispensary Arcana PDX. This industry will grow your network more than you know.

CHAPTER 14

Master of Emotion

WHETHER YOU ARE ACTIVELY WORKING on it or not, becoming a master of your emotions is an essential skill in your personal life and when selling cannabis. There will be events in your personal life that will disturb your mental health so much that it prevents you from making sales for a day or so, and that is ok. If there is something major going on in your personal life, I have found that it is best to put sales down and handle what you need to handle so you can have your complete energy and focus on generating sales. Otherwise, you will find yourself sitting behind the wheel of your car in a random parking lot, staring off in the distance, lost in thought, moving slowly through your day, not getting any healing or sales. In this chapter, I will present some instances that you will encounter in the cannabis industry where your emotional intelligence will need to be switched to the on mode.

I'm going to make this point short and sweet. There should be absolutely no fighting with anyone or anything at the beginning of your sales day. It is near impossible to have a productive sales day where your head is in the game when you start your day off with arguing and fighting. Whatever mood or feelings you start the day with tend to be the mood and feelings that you carry throughout the day. It's like putting on the socks you're wearing for the day; once you put them on and leave the house, you're going to wear them all day. If you get in the car angry, you will drive angry, manifest angering events, and show up to your appointments angry; your energy will be off, and you will not be delivering the underlying reason the purchaser works with you over your competition.

In cannabis sales you must be ready for your day to produce a combination of extreme lows followed by extreme highs, this roller coaster of emotion will transpire through various unforeseen situations. At the beginning of your cannabis sales career, you will encounter anxiety and fear more than any other emotion. You will experience these emotions every time you are going to an appointment or walking into random shops for the first time. With much certainty, I say this, you will be rejected! You will walk in, and they will ask you to go away. You will come to the end of a sales appointment and ask for the sale, and they will pass on everything you brought to sell. Without hesitation and with a smile on your face, you must say that's okay!

Some of my angriest moments were when I believed the deal was in the bag and fat commissions were on the way; then, just before the delivery, I received a phone call or text saying that they were going to hold off on their order (super painful lesson- don't count your sales chickens before they hatch). EVER!

NEVER show signs of displeasure or disappointment on your face when replying to a face-to-face rejection. If they tell you no thanks, and you make the meeting awkward by making some funky face or some disgruntled noise, you can bet your bottom dollar they will dodge you as much as they can in the future. See it from their perspective, when you tell someone no, it comes with the innate feeling of delivering disappointment and already makes the messenger feel bad. DO NOT EVER make them feel bad for telling you no, it is their job, and they can't simply purchase everything that comes in the door.

Emotional control is essential if you are going to reach the levels of success that will give you the freedom of your time and finances. In my 3rd year with Grown Rogue, I almost let my anger get the best of me and almost quit working for them; that lapse in emotional control would have cost me at least $100,000. There were some major issues with communication and the product pipeline, and it was starting to severely impact my sales commissions. After calming down and realizing my value to them and the industry, I asked the sales director to change the dynamic of our work relationship. I explained that I wanted to continue making sales for them but needed to do what was best for my future, and that I would like to be used in the capacity of a private contractor instead of being a dedicated employee. This was the most freeing thing I have ever done, and the beginning of me becoming an owner.

"Playing with my money is like playing with my emotions"-Big Worm from Friday. #FACTS. By far, one of the most frustrating and angering situations you will come across in the cannabis industry is when a company is late with their payments and does not afford you the courtesy of asking for a payment extension. Nothing makes my eyes twitch more than giving a company 15 or 30-day terms on some product (also known as a front), and when the day comes for you to pick up the payment, they don't have it. Let me list off a few excuses so that you know them when you hear them. We have payroll this week, we just paid taxes, we haven't put the product on the floor yet, the owner took all the cash, we're out of checks, we couldn't find the invoice, or when you come in to pick up payment, they inform you that they are now mailing out payments.

In the sales commission world, you don't get paid until the money is turned in, so of course, it's going to tick you. Beyond the fact that they are holding you up from getting paid, it just feels unprofessional to have money owed and to be asked by the company that you work for if you have it to turn in. So, to this I say, don't count on or have yourself in a situation where you are depending on money that is out on a front, doing so will back your emotions into a corner, and when the payment doesn't come through; like an animal backed into a corner you will only want to lash out.

Sales Hack: Payment plan- Sometimes, a debt becomes too large for a shop or business, and they will start dodging you because they payment date is near or passed and they aren't sure how to tackle the problem. Set up a meeting with whomever you have had the most communication with and come with a solution, presenting a few different payment strategies. Like a pile of dishes being ignored because it is daunting and appears to be allot of work, purchasers will be ashamed that they allowed their debt to get out of control. By providing a payment plan to help them bust down their debt, you will do much in their eyes and move from just a sales rep to an advisor.

Sales Hack: REJECTION REVERSAL- When you bring product to a dispensary, and they decide to pass on it, keep in mind that they have just brought you closer to pinpointing what they are looking to purchase. After they pass on your product/flower, ask some direct probing questions to see what they are actively hunting for when it comes to certain product/ flower or price tier/product quality tier (Top shelf, Bottom shelf). Remember that every no you receive, gets you closer to your yes! Take the rejection on the chin, keep the atmosphere happy, lighthearted, and hopeful; talk about something new that's coming that they just must check out!! This will provide comfort to the purchaser that they have not outwardly offended or hurt you and will build rapport. They will remember you and be excited the next time they see you.

CHAPTER 15

Jack of all sales

I DON'T USUALLY DISCOURAGE ANYONE from doing anything they believe they can do. But I still do not believe it wise to start your cannabis sales career representing three or more companies.

But the fact of the matter is that I don't know you, and you may possess all the self-discipline, drive, and sales competencies that it takes to be successful at being a jack of all sales. If you are reading this book before you have ever worked in sales, then you should use this chapter as an ambition of sales excellence to strive towards. This chapter is for the sales personnel that have experience selling cannabis products in their state's specific market and have built relationships within the local cannabis industry.

I say again!! Representing multiple cannabis companies is not for new sales reps and certainly not for the sloppy or lazy sales rep. You will have to deal with numerous owners with different personalities, attitudes, and expectations, along with understanding your market's specific fluctuations and having a wide customer base. You must iron out and completely understand what a company's sales expectations are when it comes to working for them, and you must know what their daily work operation expectations will be. Knowing this specific information will allow you to figure out how you will divide your time between the companies you've chosen to represent. You will have to reach whatever sales goals they expect from you and know when and how much you are to be paid. Companies with these types of employees will usually employ you as a 1099 private contractor and pay you only when your sales money is turned in. As a jack of all sales, you must consistently build your sales week prior to the week ahead, doing so will give you vision on how to split the time that is needed to get the necessary product movement for each of the companies you represent. It will be critical to implement systems like a CRM and ensure you are keeping tidy sales logs, this will help you keep track of your sales notes, appointments and all information that may be needed for reporting. Operating as a jack of all sales for an extended period is how you turn yourself from a private contractor, into a company. Representing multiple companies means you can create unlimited sales opportunities and ensure you get paid all the time; working for multiple cannabis companies equals multiple pay checks multiple times a month.

When you start selling for a company in the cannabis industry, they will undoubtedly load you up with company knowledge, product information packets, marketing pamphlets, personal samples, company swag, and trade samples for your dispensary prospects. All these different items listed above should be viewed as arrows in your opportunity quiver. Each item presents a reason for you to walk into a dispensary and have something new to present.

Before you apply to work for a cannabis company, I would perform some type of due diligence on the size of the company and its production ability. Being a jack of all sales requires you to be able to recognize if the company you have applied to is small with only a few product lines and a couple of employees dedicated to production, they might not be able to handle your sales ability. If they are a smaller company, then I suggest **NOT** signing a do not compete contract if presented. Signing a do not compete contract will limit who you are legally allowed to work for in the industry and give the cannabis company you are applying to power over who you work with, outside of them. Having the ability to sell for multiple cannabis companies grew me from an employee to an owner.

After working for a single farm for three years, I began to recognize that my value within the industry had risen significantly. Over those three years, I had built a personal brand and become an asset to anyone with a product to sell. I was known by hundreds of dispensaries purchasing managers and now possessed the ability to pull in a hundred thousand dollars in sales for anyone. This is how I became a jack of all sales. I turned myself into the go-to guy, there wasn't a cannabis product I wasn't selling, and if there was something a dispensary was hunting for and I didn't have it, I knew how to locate it. Representing multiple cannabis companies will grow your personal brand and allow your customers to know you as the sales rep that either has it or can find it. Imagine going to each dispensary you sell to with a line of cartridges, flower, extracts, and joints, that's a possibility to earn four pay checks per shop.

Heads up! One way to annoy an intake manager and get the cold shoulder is to keep trying to sell them the same flower/ cannabis products week after week. Unless something drastic changes about the product or flower you have shown them, wait a little before you bring back products they have turned down, and certainly don't bring back anything they have voiced to have an issue with. The key to being able to go back to a dispensary as many times as you want, is to always show up with a smile, have samples and something new to show them. Being a jack of all sales will help prevent your sales from becoming stale. Always bring something different or something that adds a surprise to their day, like lunch! The purchaser will get excited to see what you have brought every time, they'll never know what you will have, but will be excited to invite you to the back office and find out!

Sales Hack: Man on the inside-There will be times that the purchaser will be excited about what you have brought, but already have that strain or similar product and don't want to have competing items; so, they will pass on that basis alone. In that case, you want to keep your eye on that flower jar or product and ask questions about it! – How's it selling? How much did it cost? Have you tried it? What did you think? What do your customers think? Gather information on your competitors any chance you get! The way they speak about the product, or the vendor will let you know how close you are to replacing your competition.

Sales Hack: The key to sustained success- CRM Software- Customer relations management. As you grow your customer accounts and the variety of products that you sell, you will need a tool to help you remember all the comments, concerns, special requests, and new account leads. You NEED a CRM. These tools have become increasingly helpful by allowing you to set specific routes, track the last time you had contact with and account, take notes on what was said in the last meeting, and schedule the next time you should visit. I personally use PipeDrive and recommend it for all cannabis sales reps.

CHAPTER 16

Prepared to succeed

"If You fail to plan, then you have planned to fail"
– Benjamin Franklin

NO TRUER WORDS HAVE EVER been spoken about accomplishing sales goals or achieving after your wildest dreams! Whether you are trying to get somewhere in life, or whether you are figuring out how to get more sales, if you do not have your week planned out before it starts, you will not accomplish as much as you could. Walking into an unplanned sales week will provide two things- inefficiency and indecisiveness- both killers of your two most valuable assets.

Time and productivity.

Starting your Monday without a plan is like going to a restaurant that only has your favorite dishes on the menu. Your ability to decide on which dispensaries to visit will surely give you anxiety and cause you to drive inefficiently from one side of town to the next; instead of being systematic, you are wishfully chasing leads. Without a structured week, your mind will jump from idea to idea about which dispensary you have the best chance of making a sale with and about what you are going to sell them; this will cause you to be erratic and drive all over the place, this erratic thinking around your day is sure to reflect in the conversations with any intake managers you get in front of.

Each week you should know two things, how much you want to sell, and where you are going.

Planning out your weekly dispensary targets and deciding what you will bring them is only the beginning of setting up the weekly plan. In order to grow, you must set weekly sales goals for yourself. Just as you would obtain any large goal, you want to base your weekly sales goals off of your overall monthly sales goal.

If my monthly sales goal is $20,000/Month, then I know that my weekly sales goal breaks down into $5000/week, which in turn breaks down into a $1000/ day sales goal. This information is crucial to know before you start your week. It will drive you to more doors, help you overcome rejection, and inspire you to higher sales goals as you begin to surpass your weekly sales number.

It is important not to overwhelm yourself in the beginning. There will be enough daily nuances to get accustomed to without holding yourself mentally captive to lofty sales goals. You can set any number of goals for yourself to help you reach your monthly sales goal, just remember you must crawl before you walk.

The first six months of your cannabis sales career can be visually described by envisioning yourself trying to roll a three-hundred-pound stone, but this three-hundred-pound stone is in the shape of a cube. At first, it will take an egregious amount of effort to pick up one side and flip it to the next, and each time the stone will fall flat without an inch of forward movement. This will be your first three months of Cannabis sales, you will visit seventy shops, and you may find 1-5 shops that purchase from you consistently. These early sales have been generated from the consistent effort you are putting in day after day and your ability to connect with the dispensary purchasers quickly. It will feel like you are driving a lot without a lot of results. If you continue pushing the cube end over end, winning over another dispensary, and then another, once 3-5 months pass, you will start to notice that you have 5-10 dispensaries purchasing from you regularly and the sharp flat edges of your cube are starting to wear down and become rounded. You will notice the ease at which sales are rolling in and the strong confidence in which you enter each dispensary. Your dispensaries are now starting to reach out to you and request product drops or to ask what is new on your menu; you are starting to see consistent growth in the number of sales you generate weekly. At 6-12 months, you will notice that it is no longer a struggle to get/ find sales, and your once flat sharp-edged cube is now a smooth rounded circle in which you can push with one finger ever so slightly to gain sales momentum. This is what it is like in the beginning, lots and lots of effort for what seems to be not a lot of reward, but just remember- you must fight to gain your momentum, but once you are there the sales will seem to just roll in.

Sales Hack: One Lb, one sale, one shop per day- When you first start selling, you will start each day with hope to sell to multiple shops each day, this is first-time sales reps optimistic thought process. But as the days go on, you will notice this reality is not the case, and instead of putting your hopeful efforts into selling multiple lbs or to multiple shops a day, start off with selling one unit or lb / per day. Once you get a solid line up of reordering shops under your belt- then start shooting for selling to 2-4 shops/ day. Reaching this milestone gives you a weekly goal of 2k- 8k in sales per week- x 4 weeks, and you have a 10,000 to 20,000 at 10% commission you can START out making 1-2k/month. (Once you have momentum, you can and will sell 20k + per week. Even after five years I still use this strategy. Your market will have tuff sales months (November- December) when sales are slow and infrequent and you start to get nervous; take it back to accomplishing selling one lb, one sale, one shop per day.

Sales Hack: The sales week starts on Sunday- Momentum = progress in motion. If you are just starting to contact your dispensaries on Monday, you are behind. Sales is about momentum and in order to have the momentum you must start your week before the week starts. This effort doesn't require an entire day, but on Sunday you should be taking some time to build an attractive sales email, line up where you are going, review your sales notes, and write out your weekly sales goals. Dispensary managers parous their emails on Sunday and Monday for deals and offers to take advantage of. If you create a tantalizing email and send it on Sunday, you may get sales without even showing up, or at least sked to stop in for a sales appointment. Get your sales wheels rolling on Sunday, that way on Monday you are already going 60mph when other sales reps are just getting their engines started.

My first time in escrow. We had to fly with $700,000
cash to a bank in Colorado. This industry is full of
experiences that lie outside of dealing with cannabis.
This industry will make you a businessman or woman.

CHAPTER 17

Ask the right questions, and the money will answer

WHEN YOU WALK INTO A dispensary, you need to walk in with the confidence as if you are walking into your friend's house! Open the door like you live there, chat people up like you know them, and ask genuine open-ended questions to budtenders and customers. Every piece of information you gather grows your understanding of a shop and gets you closer to the sale, or even better, repeated sales.

Asking questions like- Is your dispensary vertically integrated? What's the most expensive gram you sell? Who is the main purchaser? May I have their email? Do you sell more top shelf or bottom shelf? What flower tier moves best for your shop? What's your fastest-moving product? Do you guys' service medical patients or have special programs? Does your shop sell more Indicas or Sativas? All of this is information you can and should gather from bud tenders. Bud tenders are the front-line fighters in the sales trenches and sometimes know the dispensary better than those that track the books. They are the forgotten asset; they will give you useful insights about the dispensary that can lead to sales! – ASK **Questions, Questions, Questions**!

Once you have done your level one internal recon, you will have enough information to generate targeted questions and build a list of items to bring for the main purchaser when you land your appointment. Don't waste your first appointment with the purchaser gathering information that you can attain from the budtenders

All shops are different and should be approached as such. It is up to you to discern what makes this specific dispensary tick! Their specific needs will be based on their city location and their consistent customer purchases. Listen intently to the buyer, **TAKE NOTES**- If you bring them what they are looking for often enough, soon you will build trust and reliability in their mind and become the person they call first when they are hunting for items for the shop. If you multiply this by 5,10, 15, 20 shops, you are now generating sales that can bring home sales commissions that equal 1,000/day. In my third year when I was private contracting for myself, I was able to put together a deal that put $3500 cash in my pocket the same day.

Sales Hack: It's not about you- When you secure a meeting with the intake manager, DO NOT go in and start

talking about yourself and what you have to offer. In the legal Cannabis market, everyone grows exceptional weed and makes exceptional products. The more questions you ask about them and the dispensary, the more information they will give you! They will feel like they are in control and speak very freely, but in reality, they are just shelling out information and tips on how you can sell to their shop, while also supplying you with subject matter on which to build rapport.

Step1 ask questions, Step2 ask questions, Step3 Shut up, listen and take physical and mental notes. You will know when to talk about yourself when they tell you what problems they must solve.

Sales Hack: Sneaky recon – I have gone into dispensaries and scoped out the shop, and when the budtender asks if they can help – I let them. Walk in with the plan of purchasing something and being seen as a customer. Ask questions about anything and everything, come off as a customer who doesn't know much about cannabis, this is how you probe for information without being recognized as a sales rep. Make sure to discernment around how busy the shop is when you walk in, if the shop is busy the budtender may feel as if they need to be urgent, and rush you through the sale. This move is for an empty shop! But always use the time you get to sneak in questions targeted on getting you information that will help lead to a sale. Remember if you're buying something, you're a customer.

CHAPTER 18

Safety Nets

ADJUSTING TO EARNING YOUR LIVING via earning sales commissions can be like navigating the open ocean. You are guaranteed to have some smooth sailing, and you are guaranteed to have some scary storms. There will be sunny months where all your sales deals will go down just the way you set them up, and opportunities you didn't even know were possible will appear out of thin air. Then, suddenly, there will be months where the waves are crashing on the deck of your vessel, your deals will fall through without warning, or they will get cut in half, and no new deals will appear.

In the world of cannabis sales, there will always be more of the unknown than pure certainty, but there are ways to guarantee some lucrative sunny days in your month. For the reason of uncertainty, one of my most valuable suggestions to you, is to find several safety net accounts/honey pots/ flotation accounts early on in your cannabis sales career. At the beginning of your

97

sales career, the sales will be spotty and very hit or miss but building a strong rapport early with a couple of shops will keep your head above water. These safety net accounts + the random sales you can generate will guarantee that you to put up some decent numbers each month. Make these your go to accounts and give them their due attention, these are accounts whom you have learned their buy cycles. They trust you and the product that you bring them. These accounts have made many purchases from you and have little to no debt and are always excited when you come around. You have the purchaser's phone # and can bring product for showing without an appointment. At these accounts, you are practically home.

Building a solid line up of these go-to accounts will ensure that you are always getting paid, and most importantly will keep you afloat when there are slow sales months.

In the beginning, you will notice that sales will come in from random accounts that you happen to drop in on, and then you will have accounts that contact you and are always checking in on your product's inventory. The ones that check in with you are your safety nets! You want to give them extra love and attention!! Showing gratitude outside of saying thank you for the sales is a smart investment! Make sure to take care of these accounts in more ways than selling them product. You need to move from their sales rep to their friend and advisor. Bring them deals that seem like they are really getting hooked up. – build a strong base of these accounts, and they will surely keep you afloat during weeks of bad sales weather.

Another safety net you should employ to help ensure sunny sales months is going after dispensary chains. Like other industries, you will find dispensaries that have multiple locations all over your state. In most cases, if you can sell to one, you will more than likely be able to sell to them all. There are two ways that dispensary chains purchase product, either through centralized buying or allowing each shop to purchase individually.

Cross your fingers for centralized buying!

This type of buying means a purchaser at a central location does the buying for all the dispensaries within the chain. Centralized buying means they are going to be purchasing their items in bulk, yielding a much higher sales ticket. In most cases, if they have you bring the items to their warehouse, they will disperse the product to their shops when they need it. This is a God send as it will keep you from having to deliver to each location around the state. Though you may be asked to deliver to each of the shops, if you are, then make sure you say yes with a smile on your face as it is guaranteed sales coming your way. The central purchaser will reach out to all dispensary managers so that they are aware you are coming and have been instructed to take the agreed-upon product at the agreed upon price. Sometimes the central buyer will pay for all the shops and sometimes you will pick up payment at each location, either way you are selling product in bulk and getting paid.

If the dispensaries purchase individually, I suggest that you get in good with one of the locations and have that manager spread the good word for you. Gaining trust and showing that your product is doing well at one of the shops will give you strong sales ground to stand on at the other locations. If your products are doing well at one location, the other locations will want to see if they can mimic the same success, products that sell fast in a dispensary make them money; and you money.

Sales Hack: Show the love, feel the love – Your safety nets are always there for you. They treat you differently, make sure they feel the same reciprocation. I have personally spent over $200 on purchasing lunch for a dispensary chain that has four shops. They purchase 30k a month with me (which I get 10% of). When the Popeyes chicken sandwich was all the rage, I would go and purchase 5-10 at a time; deliver them to almost all of the shops I did sales with; people were so thankful that I saw a spike in my sales. You can't be afraid to invest in your customer's happiness and appreciation. It will pay off in the long run. It doesn't have to be as extravagant as purchasing individual lunch for everyone, as they say; it's the thought that counts. Purchasing doughnuts or pastries for shops will have them super grateful as well. Things that come in a dozen or more are quite the perfect treat for stoners in the cannabis industry.

Sales Hack: The old Bait n Switch- You want to make sure this DOESN'T happen. When you make the sale to

a centralized buyer, they buy the quality you have presented in your sales meeting with them. If you are told to
deliver to each individual location, make sure the product pulled for your delivery matches what you showed
in your sales meeting before you leave your warehouse.
One way to get cut off from a dispensary chain is to make
the purchaser feel like you are pulling a fast one on them
by having delivering product that didn't match the quality
of what you showed in the sales meeting.

CHAPTER 19

Enough Rope To hang

THE LEGAL CANNABIS INDUSTRY IS eight years old and still
showing similarities to the wild wild west. There are loop-
holes in the rules being exploited, big bully businesses,
back door deals, businesses that are open one day and
out of business the next, all the while the entire industry
is federally illegal.

As with any new industry, you will find businesses with
eyes bigger than their budget, especially when allowed to
purchase product on terms. I have had a dispensary go
from being a great sales account that keeps up with its
purchase debt, to dodging my emails, phone calls, and
drop-in visits. In the beginning, I had a lot of trust in
dispensaries!! These are businesses, I thought to myself.
They pay their taxes and bills just like other responsible
businesses in other industries. I would let dispensaries
rack up $13,000-18,000 dollars in debt, thinking they are
a business "they will pay". Well, just like the average person who climbs into a mountain of debt and then is afraid

to face it, a few of them didn't pay. When the dispensary purchaser notices how much they owe, they tend to freak out and abruptly stop purchasing from you. Then they will start dodging all your communication attempts. They will become a headache for you, and, in turn, piss off who you're selling for. Don't let them do this to themselves, keep an eye on the dispensaries purchasing and their running balances; notice if their rope is starting to get long and cut them off!

If you notice this happen with one of your accounts, see this as an opportunity to be an advisor, and don't just immediately stop working with them. Chances are you can assist them out of their debt. You can help them get their debt back to a manageable size by proposing a small weekly payment amount that will help them chunk down their debt; don't sell to them until they have a 0 balance. If you can do this, you will be looked at as a trusted advisor, and going forward, the reason they purchase from you will extend beyond your rapport and personality.

Don't let them kill the relationship

Big sales are awesome and will put you on cloud 9, but big sales that aren't backed by big payments is the same as having a cake that you can't eat- Dumb.

COD- Cash on Delivery, a sales rep's favorite acronym! The ideal scenario is that payment is rendered the day the product is dropped off. Drop product + Receive Payment = You are earning your paycheck!! Done deal!! NEXT!!

Terms- Also known as Net, or in the black market as a front. This is when the dispensary would like to defer payment for a mutually agreed amount of time. This usually comes in the lengths of 7 days, 14 days, 31 days net. It can really be for whatever amount of time you and the shop agree to (If you are selling for someone, they may have stipulations around this). That being said, terms are a great way to get into a shop, it allows them to pick up the product without paying that day, and basically guarantees you the sale/ future paycheck.

In sales, you are paid by the money you turn in; no money turned in equals no money in your pocket. Ensure that the dispensaries you are selling to are in good financial standings, not just with you but also with other vendors. If you hear other vendors are starting to not get paid, chances are your payment will soon be delinquent; be sure to take heed to what the industry is saying.

Sales Hack: Listen to the industry. Other sales reps will inform you!! There will be rumor's and tell signs for dispensaries going out of business!! Pay attention. Businesses that go out of business don't pay. Make sure you aren't selling to a shop that is closing soon! Do their shelves look empty? Do they ever have customers when you stop by? Do they have a debt with you they just keep putting off? Look for signs that might indicate a stop selling sign.

Sales Hack: Distance amnesia- Be mindful when giving terms to dispensaries you visit on road trips. It is easy for them to forget/ put off paying you due to the distance. Also, it can be hard to get out to distant shops when you have a big local route. For me, anyone more than an hour drive must pay COD, or at least 50% down.

CHAPTER 20

Road Warrior

IN THE PAST FIVE YEARS, I have driven around the entire state of Oregon in search of homes for cartridges, extracts, edibles, and pounds of flower. I have sold cannabis products in every major city and most of the small ones. Depending on how many sales reps your company has, there may be untapped sales territory outside of your current city/ territory. Once you have a good grasp on the products you're selling, hitting the road in search of sales is a great way to break up your sales schedule. Sales trips can be a fun business adventure, you just have to go with the right mindset. Treating your road sales as an adventure is a major hack for getting work done while maximizing the fun.

I have taken 3-day road trips where I stayed in hotels all three days, and other times I have camped under the stars. I always bring my frisbee golf disks and bowling balls in hopes of playing a new course or alley along my trip. Whatever you enjoy doing in your hometown can likely be enjoyed on the road. If you keep the sales road trips fun for yourself, you will never feel as if you're working, and if you can land a bunch of sales while you are making it fun, you will think this isn't real life.

Though being out on the road visiting new towns and dispensaries is a fun adventure, the overall goal is to either bring in sales or start building the relationships that lead to sales. I have found that there are critical pre-trip steps to take that will ensure a safe and successful sales road trip. Following these steps will allow for a smooth take-off, travel, and landing.

1. Where are you headed? Pin down the last dispensary you plan on stopping at in your road trip. Now you will be able to see every dispensary between your starting point and finishing. Doing this will allow you to build your route and start building time estimations for the places you plan to visit.

2. Once you know the dispensaries you plan to visit, give them a call or send an email trying to lock in an appointment. Let them know you will be traveling to see them and ask what type/ price of products suit their shop best. QUESTIONS, QUESTIONS!! Get all info that might help you land the sale at the first meeting. Anyone that you lock in an appointment with gets the priority on the trip, whatever day and time you have said you would be there, make sure that you are

there; even if you have to skip some of the shops you planned on stopping at but didn't hear from.

3. Once you lock in your appointments and know what they want, you should start building your product line of items you believe will bring you the most success. Usually bringing a variety is best, bring the expensive, bring the mids, and bring the cheap. This will guarantee you bring something for everyone and have a higher opportunity of getting multiple sales.

4. One thing that is major but often overlooked is what time you plan on being at your first dispensary. Get your sales trip started on the right foot by having all your needed items checked and ready to go. The night prior, you should have your bags packed, car packed with a full gas tank, do a car inspection that includes oil levels, tire air levels, windshield wiper check. The product you will be showing should already be on a manifest, and the manifest should already be printed and waiting on top of your transportation bins. The only thing you should need to do in the morning is pick up your product from your wholesale, or just head out if you already have your product with you.

5. Be sure to set up reservations at any hotels you wish to stay at and have an idea where you will be sleeping at the end of your days on the road. You don't want to get caught in a situation where

everything is either closed or has 0 vacancies. Other scenarios could make this a point of anxiety if you don't have it mapped out.

6. Road trips are not guaranteed to make money but are guaranteed to cost money. If finances are tight, I don't recommend hitting the road in search of Gold. There is any number of scenarios that could happen out on a sales road trip that might require you to come out of pocket right on the spot. Don't allow yourself to get caught on the side of the road with no money and no cell phone service.

On my very first trip, I knew I wanted to be on the road for 3 days, but I didn't nail down some very crucial details, like where I would be staying along the way or what time I wanted to arrive. At the end of my second day, I found myself at the end of a 13 hr sales day on the Oregon coast with the rain coming down so hard I couldn't make out the lines on the road. Absolutely exhausted and feeling sleepy, I look up "hotels near me". The closest hotel was over an hour away.

If you have never seen the Oregon Coast, it is beautiful... and full of cliffs that lead to the cold blue Ocean.

Being on the road for several days at a time requires vision, the ultimate win on a sales trip is bagging sales, you will limit this opportunity if you are having to use valuable time to figure out where you will sleep, or worst broken down on the side of the road.

If you were planning a road trip to visit the Grand Canyon, would you go without planning? How many days ahead would you prepare? What time of day should you leave? What are all the things you will need to bring, clothes, gear? Are you going to check over your vehicle? What is the most optimal route?

These are just a few questions that you will need to answer before you get on the road for a sales road trip. It is pertinent that you have this all planned out at least a week before you plan to hit the road. If you don't plan your trip out as much as possible, you will find yourself scrambling around the morning you are supposed to take off; setting you back at least an hour from when you planned to take off. This will immediately cut into the number of shops you can visit the first day. When traveling to dispensaries that are far away, you must make the most of the time available for catching intake managers while they are in shop, which happens to be 9-4.

Unless you are told that you must stay in a specific sales territory, I highly recommend visiting the dispensaries and companies on the outskirts of the state. In weed sales, your money is at the dispensaries. Always be willing to go get it!

When I recognized the farm I was working for company only had two sale reps, me and another guy, I immediately started getting excited about the possibility of big sales in small towns and started planning a trip. The problem with planning for something you've never done is that until you've done it a couple of times, you will be learning. Apply the tips I've given above, and your learning curve will be shorter.

Sales Hack: Head out Monday- Every dispensary needs to order something on Monday, if you have a sales trip planned, I recommend leaving on a Monday. Hitting long distance shops on a Monday will give you better chance of showing up when their wallets are open, and they have holes to fill. Showing up later in the week will give them the opportunity to stock up on items they could have purchased from you. Cannabis sales is about relationships and TIMING.

Sales Hack: Get paid- Depending on how far out you drive and the time in which you plan to return, it is always best practice to have dispensaries pay COD for their purchase; especially when you are far from home base. If it's not easy to plan a return trip, be mindful of allowing terms for sales. You only get paid for the money you turn in.

One of my first solo trim deals representing myself.
This is probably only about 800-1,000 lbs, pretty small
compared to the 2,500lb deals we do today.

CHAPTER 21

Head On A Swivel

Since 1971 and the introduction of the war on drugs, cannabis has become a highly sought-after drug that people have had no problem killing for. America's war on drugs created a mass scarcity of cannabis, raising its demand and giving the drug high street value. The street value of cannabis has given it the ability to be expensive and retain the ability to be sold fast. I believe one of the best outcomes of legalized cannabis is the accessibility it has provided to its consumers. This accessibility has lowered the overall scarcity of cannabis and the extremes people are willing to go to obtain it. I haven't heard of anyone killing for corn or potatoes, and I hope Cannabis will be able to fall into that category one day.

But let's be real, people kill for money and drugs every day.

Boiled down to its main components, the legal cannabis industry consists of money and drugs. If you choose this career path, you must be prepared for any scenario. Truthfully, selling cannabis legally isn't far off from the conditions of selling it illegally. You are dealing with lots of money and lots of weed, and unfortunately, people will always want what you have.

Always keep your head on a swivel!!

There are two items that I will discuss below that I suggest you employ for your safety and the protection of your credibility. I must start by saying I have not and do not currently employ these items personally within Oregon, but when national sales become possible, I will.

My only legitimate excuse for my lack of safety preparedness is that Oregon is a different cannabis playground than all other states. In Oregon, everyone and their mother has either been growing or making cannabis products for 20+ years. There is so much cannabis available in the Oregon market that five-dollar eighths can be found at most dispensaries.

Fact- there are more dispensaries in Portland proper than McDonalds and Starbucks combined. To say the least, weed is everywhere.

This is not to say it can't happen here or to me, but in my five years of being in the legal market, I have not heard of any sales reps being robbed in Oregon. However, I have heard of dispensaries being robbed at gunpoint and even one situation where a budtender was shot.

As I have stated in previous chapters, you must protect two things in this industry, yourself and your reputation.

1. Protecting yourself

Now I know a bunch of you will think to yourself, "I know how I'll protect myself; I'll just ride with a pistol or bring a self-defense weapon." However, keep in mind that if you bring it, you intend to use it. If you bring a gun or weapon, you are saying to the universe that you are ready to get into a shootout over some weed. You are willing to put the one life you get on the line over a product that can be insured and grown repeatedly in repetitive cycles.

Can your life be grown again?

I do not and have not carried a gun for this very reason. If you get into a stick-up situation, remain calm and give them the product and the money. Both can be recouped and replaced... your life cannot. You must go into a stickup situation with this relaxed mindset, so you still have a life to move forward with.

I do feel you should be able to protect yourself if you ultimately need to do so, and in this case, I have a pepper spray gun in my vehicle. Don't let someone force you into a vehicle or into a hostage situation; remind them that they are there for the weed and money, not you. I don't want to kill, nor be killed for cannabis. Therefore, I have the pepper spray gun to use if necessary. The plan is to blind them and get away- finishing the situation with my life is a win in my book.

2. Protect your trust/ reputation-

Imagine if you will- (GUN IN YOUR FACE) Give me all your cash and your fucking weed totes!

Calming your emotions from that nerve-wracking situation will take some time, and unfortunately, you will soon have to relive the whole situation many times over. Once you explain the whole situation to your company, they will file a police report in which you will have to explain the whole situation to a police officer. More than likely, you will have to give a statement to several different officers/ agents and the owners of the company you work for.

If you are robbed for product or money, your word and reputation will immediately be on the line. No matter how much product or money was stolen, you will have a lot of thorough explaining to do. Providing strong evidence that you had nothing to do with the robbery will go a long way in protecting your freedom and reputation. Unfortunately, without strong evidence, there will be a small voice in your employer's mind saying that you might have had something to do with it. For this very reason, I suggest sales reps purchase two things.

Body Cam and **Car Cam**. Utilizing these pieces of safety equipment will go a long way in exonerating you from any implications that may be floating around. I have investigated both cameras and found that you can get a good body camera and car camera on Amazon for around $99-$150 each. With these two items in play, you can provide concrete evidence that may help your company recover its product and money, but most importantly you will be protecting your reputation within the industry.

Below I have listed the actions I have taken to ensure my safety week after week.

Sales Hack: Park in the front- There are cameras all around the front of all dispensaries, and people are usually walking in and out; always park where you can see at least one camera facing you. This will make anyone with bad intentions think twice before making a move on you.

Eye Contact- When you step out of your car, look around and see if anyone is watching you. Anytime I have noticed suspicious persons watching or staring, I make sure to stare them in the eyes and let them know that I see them. Anyone that knows they have been spotted will feel like you may know what they are up to and may deter them from making a move.

Ask for a walkout- Dispensary managers will usually have no issue with giving you a walkout to your car. No need to be too proud to ask. Be sure to ask for an escort to your car If it is dark out or if a dispensary is in a sketchy area of town. Your safety should be a high priority for the dispensary.

Sales Hack: Schedule rotation- never visit the same set of dispensaries in a set time on a set day of the week. Change your weekly routes and times that you visit shops. By not being predictable, you are making it difficult for anyone to plan an attack.

Tinted windows- A thief won't get tempted by what they can't see. You must hide / conceal all your cannabis items. I use a 5% tint on my back windows and 10% tint on the driver and passenger windows. Make sure to especially hide the black and yellow totes from plain sight. These bins are starting to become synonymous as cannabis bins.

CHAPTER 22

Market Eb and Flow that will fuck with your hustle

OVER THE PAST SEVEN YEARS, there has been a noticeable trend developed by states that have brought the legal cannabis industry to life. Most states that provide recreational cannabis started by taking the medicinal approach to legalization. Once a state has crossed this threshold, they will watch and grow their understanding of this new industry for about a year or two, then after this time of information gathering, they will vote for a transition over to a full recreational cannabis program. Offering cannabis medicinally before providing it recreationally allows the state to begin outlining the necessary details of the infrastructure for its state-run cannabis regulation agency. The state must outline the required taxes, rules and regulations, business licensing, packaging requirements, and many other nuances of this new industry.

Due to the federal government's current drug scheduling of cannabis, states have had to tread carefully to understand the federal government's requirements of State-run cannabis programs. I do believe that our federal government is taking a similar approach before allowing for national legalization. Right now, they are doing their homework by seeing what works and doesn't from state to state, figuring out the best way and at what rates to tax, and deciding what agency will oversee regulating the industry (I believe it will be the ATF)

Industries in their infantile stage provide little to no empirical data on the possible behavior, growth, or overall direction of that industry. Cannabis has always been in high demand and has had its own market since the creation of this country. Since the rapid legalization across the United States has taken place, it has been relatively easy to recognize trends that form in the beginning of most states legal market.

Depending on how your state chooses to doll out its licenses, and your state's ability to provide outdoor growing, you will begin to see trends in price and flow within year two or three. Oregon has just entered the fifth year of its recreational cannabis industry and has some well-defined trends that have appeared every year since the beginning. Due to our high influx of outdoor flower each year, price of all products falls in November and raise in the summer.

From state to state, weed can be produced differently, whether indoor, full sun outdoor, light assisted outdoor, or greenhouse. These different methods of growing weed are dictated by the states' naturally provided climate and geography, each growing practice produces different quantities and qualities of Cannabis. Most Indoor farms can produce anywhere from 50 to several hundred lbs per harvest, this month-to-month harvesting is called "perpetual harvest, growing indoors allows the grower to control the harvest cycle time and conditions.

In order to grow full sun outdoor flower or light dep (light deprived) flower, the state's climate must provide consistent sunny summer months from May to October, but having sunny days is merely the tip of the iceberg for being able to grow cannabis outdoors. You must also have enough water available and know that there aren't other inclement weather conditions that could ruin your entire crop- i.e. Tornadoes, Freak snow storm, hail storm, locust swarm etc. For these reasons, Oregon and Northern California can grow the most outdoor flower of any state in the United States, this abundant ability to frow outdoors has given southern Oregon and Northern California the token name "The Emerald Triangle". In Oregon our outdoor grows can produce anywhere from 2,000 to 10,000 lbs of usable product each harvest, which happens once a year in October. This consistent annual harvest combined with the number of outdoor farms has prompted Oregonians in the cannabis industry to recognize October as Croptober. If your state produces any full sun outdoor, light Dep, or greenhouse, you can bet that you will see similar price fluctuation trends during certain times of the year.

The Oregon market is what I believe to be the most volatile recreational cannabis market in America, due to the massive allotment of cannabis producer licenses issued and the amount of cannabis that is able to be grown annually, we have started to notice that the supply is outweighing the demand. There are currently over 1300 (down from 2,000) farms/ producer licenses, over 700 dispensaries, 600 wholesales, and 300 extractors within a state with four million residents. I'm sure some of you have read news articles about the gross overages of weed grown in Oregon's legal market. This gross oversupply of cannabis has caused the price of some outdoor flower to fluctuate down to 0.22 cents per gram, at that gram price you are looking at a pound price of $100. Though most markets will start off small and limited, you can guarantee as we start to look towards some form of national legalization, most markets/ if not the whole country will mirror the growth of the Oregon market.

Each state's individual market will develop a normalcy for where its prices usually dwell. If prices start to rise or drop within your market, you should start asking yourself questions to figure out the root cause. You must recognize **WHEN** and **WHY** prices have fluctuated in your market. Any time price fluctuates, this means there has been a change in the supply, price drops usually indicate some type of oversupply or price hikes indicate an undersupply. Figure out why the supply has changed; will it be annual? biannual? quarterly? If you can recognize this change to happen on any type of regularity, you should begin to strategize your sales tactics before the change. In order to get sales, your product must be close to market price; if the market price adjusts, you must adjust.

When it comes to new cannabis markets, I have noticed a simple and predictable flow of supply, demand, and price. All industries are driven heavily by the supply and the demand for that supply, it makes sense that the cannabis market is no different. Below I have outlined a flow that most state cannabis programs will go through, license issuance will have its greatest effect on supply, demand and price starting around year three.

Year One and Two- Consumers are through the roof excited. There are waiting lines wrapped around dispensaries that are hours long, the prices of the flower and other cannabis products will be equal to street value, if not more. Buying weed from the store and trying new products will be all the craze. There will be such a demand for cannabis by the consumer that the few shops that are open will run into the issue of running out of cannabis products and will possibly resort to allowing cannabis purchases via appointment only. Cannabis, like any other plant, takes time to be grown. Once harvested, farmers must wait the full pre-determined amount of time before they are able to harvest again.

Year Three and Four- The excitement about the industry has calmed a little, dispensaries have regulars and have noticed monthly sales trends within the shop. The market supply has started to catch up with the demand, dispensaries are able to keep their shops supplied with cannabis products and prices will lower slightly. This is when the issuance of licenses and your state's ability to provide outdoor flower or light dep will begin to have the greatest effect on the markets supply and trends presented by this supply.

Sales Hack: The coldest time of year- The end of the year (End of Nov-December) will always be the most difficult time of year to sell. During this time there are conditions outside of supply that have a great effect on cannabis sales, this is where demand takes the front seat. This end of year sales trend shows up in the dispensaries sales and in the ability to make sales to dispensaries.

1. Sales inside the dispensary. Christmas- never underestimate the consumers need to redirect some of their cannabis funds to purchasing gifts for their loved ones. Dispensaries tend to see slower sales because the consumers weed budget will be shared with gift purchases, slower weed moving inside the dispensary means lower amounts of cannabis needed to keep up with the consumers' demand.
2. Sales to the dispensary- Taxable product- At the end of the year dispensaries are taxed on the product they have in their stock, most shops limit

the amount of product they purchase through-out the month, as not to be caught with a ton of taxable product on hand. You will literally see a massive uptick in sales the first week in January.

Sales Hack: Talk to the market- Everyone in your industry is a wealth of information, from the budtenders to the purchasers, to the owners and other sales reps. Verifying market conditions will come from the market conversations that you have with the constituents that are within your industry. If you go to ten different dispensaries and ask the same question, you will start to notice some consistencies in the answers- once you notice the consistencies, you have found useful information. Each year when I notice prices rising or lowering, I begin poking around for answers by asking different people if they are hearing of or coming across any crazy low/ high prices or if they are having difficulty finding certain products. Depending on the answers I get, I will start to draw conclusions on where the market is headed, and about how long the condition I am noticing; turns drastic.

CHAPTER 23

Fall in Love with
the Process

As I AM DEALING WITH and understanding the loss of my
mother, I have concluded that life is one big learning lesson and that can be broken down into smaller lessons
spread out over your entire life. The reason for human
existence has been a question on my mind lately, and
I believe that reason is to learn, adapt, and pass it on.
I know that seems to cut and dry as I have tried to explain the reason for human life in a short sentence, but
what is for sure is that life has a way of making sure we
learn the lessons one way or another. Life has a funny
way of throwing the same lesson into your path again and
again, hoping someday you will grow from it and then
tell someone else how to handle that exact lesson. I have
come to understand that some lessons can't be avoided
or dodged, some lessons are handed to us so that we may
learn how to handle life better; like the death of a loved

one, unavoidable, but on the other side of the pain there are healthy ways to handle and grow from it.

Our entire life is a damn learning process, and you got to fall in love with it babbbyyyy! All the ups, all the downs, all the crazy, all the strange, it's all about how you handle your experiences that shape the story of your life and your perception of the world. When it boils down to it, the process and the lessons of your life; Is just your life. Love every moment of every day.

If you are new to the cannabis industry, you will need to rack up some work experiences until you find the sector where you thrive the most. I have had friends start in the sales side and find that they would much rather be doing the farming side. I have a superstar sales rep who worked as a budtender for four years, and now prefers being on the road bouncing from shop to shop and getting paid via sales commissions. Truth is, you won't know how much you will like or dislike a particular avenue in the cannabis industry until you try it. But whatever you try, try your best and catalogue all the knowledge and experiences you gain. I can truly say that I am a great sales rep because I have worked in every avenue the cannabis industry offers. I have helped grow, worked as a budtender, worked in product production and become very comfortable at sales (I have sold every type of cannabis product in the industry). I have allowed myself to try everything, knowing that I would stumble upon what I loved most and that every work experience was only developing my love and passion for the cannabis industry.

Now my passion and love for the industry spews out in every sales meeting I have. With every ounce of confidence, I can say I can connect with any purchaser at any cannabis company, in any state. Everyone I speak to is made hungry from my passion, even these words are merely a transformation of my passion into something tangible.

Cannabis sales are fun but are also built on grueling, long, hot, cold, and rainy days. This position is not for those without resilience, patience, imagination, or who are unwilling to learn new lessons and fall in love with every challenge. You will have to talk yourself into continuing day after day, having faith that sunnier sales days are around the corner. Developing a deep love and understanding of the cannabis industry as a whole is pertinent if you are considering being a sales rep, that love and passion will carry you through your hard days and help you gain valuable perspective for who you want to be in the industry.

Yes, I am a cannabis sales rep at heart, but that's not my end. I now see that all my sales and road traveling experience has prepared me for my next chapter in Cannabis, leading my own cannabis sales team and being on the road for book sales and teaching workshops.

I hope I have been very clear throughout this book on the difficulties and challenges of choosing to be a sales rep, especially in the beginning. I believe the toughest challenge is to have faith that your success as a sales rep is coming; and keep the consistency with the tasks that will get you there. DO NOT make it about the money. This may be the desired outcome and even driving force but make it five or six on your reason for being a cannabis sales rep list. Sales is too challenging, and the money can be too inconsistent in the beginning to make it about the money. I believe that if you commit to giving your all for six months in cannabis sales, you will begin to find the consistency, passion, and success you started out looking for; in turn, these three will give you the ability to be paid more than you ever have. Six months is where I saw the biggest change for myself and many other sales reps, but you have to be all in and put in the work to get your desired results.

Sales Hack: Study Cannabis- One way to connect with anyone in the cannabis industry is to be able to talk about all things cannabis. Working in industry will intrinsically allow you to develop knowledge of all things cannabis through conversations with people from different sectors and learning the products. Through these conversations, you will begin to develop a broad understanding of the plant and the many different effects it has on the human body. I recommend creating a notebook and looking up scientific information about cannabis and the ECS so that you may be able to have strong, genuine conversations with anyone in the industry.

Sales Hack: Work as a budtender- I don't usually recommend people work as budtenders as the position tends to have quite the low sealing for growth but working as

a budtender can take your cannabis game to another level. Every sector's job in cannabis is to produce something to be sold within the dispensary. Therefore, if you learn the ins and outs of the dispensary, you will be better equipped to sell dispensaries cannabis products. My six months working as a budtender allowed me to see all the details that make a dispensary tick, from their purchasing processes, how items are moved within the shop, and even how the average budtender thinks from shop to shop. All of these details helped me better understand the dispensary, and in turn have helped me in selling to dispensaries.

You must start somewhere. This was my first wholesale. I rented
space from another wholesale, clearly not enough room.

Space is always an issue.

"SuperSacks" one time we were sent 2,000lbs for oil processing and it came in bags so big we couldn't fit them in the door. Thankfully I have a great team that helped me rebag them in about 3 hrs. This bag is 247lbs.

CHAPTER 24

Everyone is an Asset

I CAN'T BE ANY CLEARER about this. The cannabis industry is completely and utterly about networking. Your state industry will start off small, and everyone will know everyone, if you do something shady or produce bad business, the word will get out, and you will be quietly blacklisted. You must avoid burning bridges at all costs and ensure your character is protected within every deal. You don't want to be branded for negative business issues. If so, you can bet your well of connections will dry up, no one will want to work with you, and the money will stop flowing in.

I encourage you to make friends, trade contact info, and hang out with all sales reps you meet. Other sales reps are not the enemy and usually not your direct competition, and if they are your competition, you should get to know them even more (keep your friends close and your enemies closer). You NEED to be making friends like your paycheck depends on it. There have been dispensaries I was unable to get a sale at for over a year, then one day on a drop-in visit, I found out that the intake manager has left and now the budtender that I have been chatting with and becoming friends with over the past year is now the person in charge of purchasing; turning that shop from a no-buy zone, to a money tree.

I have become great friends and allies with people that would be considered my competition, from running into them time and time again at different dispensaries. Fast forward a couple of years, and now we help each other move and find flower, a lot of times to the same customers.

The Cannabis Industry is filled with three types of people.

The content Stoner-People who just outright love cannabis but don't view the industry as their rocket ship to life transformation. They have knowledge of growing, smoke regularly, love the plant for all of its attributes and abilities, and love working with people and cannabis, which keeps them satisfied.

The Mogul- Usually the owner or where the funds come from. Business infrastructure oriented, views the cannabis industry as a billion-dollar market that they want a portion of. In and out of the shop behind the scenes, never a budtender. Their purpose and reason for being in the industry is the almighty dollar.

The Stoner Mogul- These people are the industry hustlers making the companies they work for or own, industry competitors. They are in and out of all the shops!! They know everyone from the Budtenders to the Owners. They partake in cannabis when they can and attend industry events. They are business savvy stoners that are always hungry for growing their passion with new partnerships, bigger deals, and the belief in the future of cannabis.

Everyone's approach to the market comes with their own varying level of importance and access to different aspects of the cannabis industry. Knowing how different individuals perceive the market is important for gathering information and pursuing interests, you will begin to categorize people and recognize what information and use they are best suited.

When you get into the industry, you will have to answer a personal question-

What type of person am I in this industry? How soon do I want to be?

We're all in it for different reasons, but we all need each other. The recreational cannabis industry is built up of money, friends, and cannabis.

In every industry, information and contacts are king. This industry is no different. Your first four months, you will get some sales right away, and some you will have to gather more and more information until you build the trust and bring them exactly what they are looking for!

Sales Hack: Chatty Kathy- RELATIONSHIPS! You should be meeting and making new relationships weekly. Talk to every product vendor you pass in shops and exchange info; get the phone number for every owner you meet! Your Network is truly = Net worth. DO NOT IGNORE! Other people can make you money or bring money making opportunities to your door.

Sales Hack: Budtender soldiers- Bud Tenders sell your product, they are the sales reps within the dispensary, if you want them to sell your product; you must get them samples! Why? Because they are the ones selling your product, I can repeat it again if you need. Budtenders will push products they know and have tried; the number one question customers ask is "Have you tried it?" If they can't say yes, then the customer is less likely to take a chance on trying your product; and that's your fault. If you want your product to sell fast in any dispensary, load them up with samples. Plus, everyone loves gifts, if the bud tenders notice you are taking care of them because they are always receiving samples from your company, you will grow their perception of you and your product. GET THEM SAMPLES!

Some heavenly looking crumble extract. Just needs to be
individually weighed and jarred; then it's ready to be sold.

CHAPTER 25

Be a Creator

THE ONLY CONSTANT IN LIFE is change, and the cannabis industry is a shining beacon of that truth. In 1973
the United States declared cannabis a schedule one
drug and prohibited its possession and use throughout the country. Harsh punishments followed these
laws, innately stripping away any ability to learn about
Cannabis and its effects on the body. Forty-Five years
later- Washington State and Colorado became the first
states to allow their residents to vote for legalizing cannabis for the residents of these states. 2015 was the birth
year of the legal cannabis industry, bringing in the rush
for green gold.

Since the birth of the legal cannabis industry, I have
watched the products that have weed in them evolve from
one level to the next. From regular joints, to now triple
infused joints with kief, wax, and oil, to isolating THC
down into its molecule form called THCA- Crystallin
(Looks like Meth)- is almost pure THC at 98-99%. As

much as I love an old-fashioned joint or smoking a bowl out of a glass pipe or bong, I cannot deny the beautiful metamorphosis of this industry and the unique spectrum of products that cannabis has been melded into.

I started in the legal cannabis industry as a sales rep for a single farm, then became a private contractor representing multiple cannabis companies, then started a wholesale representing farms, extractors, and edible producers for my own business. Now I own a dispensary, wholesale, and processing license. This industry is all about growth, growing your customers, growing your brand, growing your network, growing your capacity; You should never be still for too long, your evolution will always be around the corner if you push for it.

It is beautiful to know this industry is in its infantile stages, one in which we haven't even begun to see the full growth potential nor the people that are going to be the leaders of this industry. Companies are going under every day; just as new cannabis companies are opening their doors. With our industry still in the infancy stages, I implore you to think outside the box and create new items, more efficient processes, and new ancillary companies. The biggest reason I am writing this book is that there are currently 0 books or YouTube videos on the nuances of Legal cannabis sales. I am looking into the not-so-distant future and seeing national legalization and multitudes of people searching for a tool to help them grow within this budding industry.

Sales Hack: Stir the Imagination- There are a ton of books on sales that will provide useful information to help you grow as a sales rep but be sure to learn information outside of sales. Stir your imagination with learning knowledge of self-growth, and of different industries, you never know what new perspective will hatch from the intake of new information, it could produce the idea for your own cannabusiness.

Sales Hack: Pans and Shovels- The Cannabis industry is supported by hundreds of ancillary industries, from plastics, fabrics, printing and marketing, and accounting just to name a few; and we are in need of more. Think of a company/ product you can create that would add major support / valuable need within the Cannabis industry. It's not all about starting a Cannabis business. The support businesses are just as lucrative and important. More people got rich selling pans and shovels to gold prospectors than those that went and searched for the gold.

Green Gold- When you squeeze oranges, you get orange
juice. When you squeeze weed, you get gold.

CHAPTER 26

Make money anywhere

ONE THING I LOVE MOST about cannabis sales, is once the proper channels are set up, the way you can earn money has a strong resemblance to passive income. As I have said throughout this book, time is your most valuable asset. In the beginning you will spend allot of it running around chasing leads, following up, and building your relationships. Once your relationships are solidified, you will have the ability to make money from your phone a laptop and a beach.

Truth of the matter is, you need to be able to sell to your dispensary partners without always having to physically show up, this is the only way you will be able to grow your sales. If you are only able to sell to them when you are physically there, when will you have the time or capacity to cultivate new dispensaries? Earning the implicit trust of your dispensaries is the only way for this to be a possibility, they must know they can order from you and their order will arrive when it's supposed to, how its supposed to, and if there are ever any issues you will make sure they are squared away immediately. When a dispensary orders product, they want to receive it, then get it out on the shelves for their customers, especially if this is a product their customers have come to know and love and its missing from their shelves.

The overall goal for any purchaser is to simplify their purchasing, they want to be able to get the products their customers know and love without having to speak with a sales rep each time. Cartridges, edibles, extracts, and joints are items easily purchased from a menu list, once the purchaser has come to know and have faith in the brands behind these products, they will order freely to ensure there isn't gap of time the product is missing from the shelf, if you sell any of these items at a certain point you will see sales just roll in without hearing a word from the purchaser.

Selling flower without physically being there can be a tad bit trickier, flower is more of an individual experience each time and is by far one of the most expensive items that a dispensary purchase. Experienced farmers can produce similar quality flower results from harvest to harvest, but throughout each harvest there are a plethora of issues that can affect the quality, changing the outcome of the flower. Most purchasers are going to want to look over the quality of the trim on the buds, smell the nose permeating from the flower, see what the THC tests at and possibly negotiate on the price. But have no fear it is not impossible to sell flower without being physically present, again this will roll back to trust in the brand/ farm and you. Once the trust is built and you're able to have flower dropped off without being present, you must now be prepared for the day that something is delivered, and the dispensary is not pleased with the product. When, not If this happens (it will happen at least once) you must be prepared to go to all lengths of customer service in order to remedy the situation. There are a few options if a dispensary is not pleased with the product being delivered, you can reach out to your farm to ask for a discount, you can have backup options for replacement (try and keep it in similar type and price), and sometimes you may just have to inform your farm the flower is coming back. Whatever action is required to be able to keep the trust, is what you must do. Trust is like a glass vase, once it breaks if you can put it back together, it will have cracks all throughout it; if they ever feel tricked or like they are getting the raw end of the deal, you can be sure that if you sell flower there again, you will have to be there in person.

In this book I only teach you what I know and what I have tried, when built correctly; you really can make money from anywhere.

For the first three years of my sales career, I sold for one farm, every dispensary that knew me, knew that I sold for Grown Rogue and had come to know and trust all flower they produced. In the beginning of 2020, I was preparing to go on a two-week vacation to Costa Rica, I was still working for this farm and had begun selling for a few different brands as well, I knew I could sell to over half my shops without even showing up. Before going I purchased an unlimited international data plan and calling plan, purchased a new I-Pad, and planned to wake up early and work for 2-3 hours in the morning each day. I informed all my dispensaries that I wouldn't be popping in for a couple weeks, but that I would still send them menus and would set up delivery for any product they wanted. While on vacation I was able to sell $140,000 dollars in product to at least 20 different cannabis businesses, I sold several thousand pounds of trim, several hundred pounds of flower, and several thousand grams of extracts, all from pool side at Airbnb's, beaches, and a variety of cafes. At the end of my vacation, I was able to return home with more money than when I started.

Sales Hack: Set the boundary- As sales reps, we love to have our cake and eat it to, but if you don't hold boundaries with how much you work, it can be damaging to your personal relationships. If you plan on getting some work in on vacation, make sure you set up designated work times, that you don't break. If you are on vacation with family or friends and in a time zone that allows, try to wake up early before anyone else and get your work in, then when work time is supposed to be over; let it be over. It is easy to fall in love with making money, but money isn't everything

Sales: Protect what you have earned- Once you get to the point that you are making sales without having to be physically present, be careful because there is a trap waiting for you. It's called complacency. You will think that you have that account locked in the bag and if they are receiving

their orders and the product is selling on their shelves, that your relationship is great; but you could be losing some of your shelf space to a newcomer who is growing their relationship with the purchaser. Relationships require time and effort, make sure you are visiting the shop even if its just to drop off some treats and say hello; continuing to do vendor days shows that you care about their dispensary, put in the effort. Account relationship maintenance is necessary for you to hold the relevancy and strength of what got you on the shelf in the first place, with a strong relationship you can keep other similar products from encroaching on your shelf territory.

Our first product line. The first 10 full gram
joint pack to the PDX market.

CHAPTER 27

The Virus and recession-proof Industry

NOTHING IN LIFE IS KNOWN. If you were to tell me that in 2020 Kobe Bryant would die, that it would be the beginning of an International Pandemic and there would be International civil protests, I would ask you what horror movie you were talking about.

But all of that has happened, and for the next two years there was no end in sight.

As I am writing this book, we are entering the second year of the Covid-19 pandemic and there have been multiple strains of Covid 19 surface. Everyone is wearing masks, vaccines and booster shots are being pushed like stimulus checks, businesses have closed that will never open again, and the unemployment rate has risen exponentially. Companies have laid off employees due to not knowing when they will open their doors again or transitioned them to working from home full time, and hundreds of thousands of people are praying that the government doles out another stimulus check.

The cannabis Industry on the other hand is thriving, more dispensaries are opening all over the country, six more states have legalized cannabis recreationally, and tax revenue for the cannabis industry nationally is already well over a billion dollars. Locally, some of my partner dispensaries have reported a 20-30% increase in sales, all while being open for limited hours and battling long lines due to social distancing rules. At the beginning of the pandemic Oregon created a list of industries that they deemed to be essential, with their employees being deemed essential workers were permitted to continue working, surprisingly enough the cannabis industry found its way onto the essential list and was permitted to keep providing cannabis to consumers. Oregon was not alone in this initiative of granting essential workers status to their cannabis industry, eight other states also deemed the cannabis industry to be essential and permitted them to stay open for business. So, while companies that you and I have known for years had to shut their doors, the cannabis industry has expanded to new legal heights.

I believe the great depression was a great indicator of the type of industries that thrive when times are tough, in tough times people are going to be looking for a mental escape in whatever way it comes and will spend their dollars for their preferred escape even if they have little to no money. During the great depression, alcohol and tobacco sales skyrocketed to new heights creating a visual of the economic prosperity possible through these industries, their economic stimulation helped move alcohol out of its illegal status to the acceptance we have for it today, and I can see the same thing happening with cannabis. The cannabis industry has grown in the face of an economic downturn and an international pandemic, bringing about a lifeline of economic stimulus to individual States at a most crucial time.

Sales Hack: Secure your future- Are you in an industry that closed its doors at the beginning of the pandemic? Do you love cannabis? Make the transition! This industry is new and booming and in search of great thinkers with great talent. Don't be put out of work because your industry isn't deemed essential, cannabis has already been given essential status and you can bet that if anything similar happens in the future; our doors will remain open.

Sales Hack: Not sure if you should get into the Cannabis industry? Apply this quote to how you feel about where you are currently working, and how you feel about transitioning to this new and booming industry. "If it scares you then you already know, and if it doesn't then it's time to go" – Benjamin Richardson. Growth always appears scary, but what's scarier is waking up in ten years and being exactly in the same place.

CHAPTER 28

Puzzle Masters

IN ITS ESSENCE, THE LEGAL cannabis industry is simple. We drive, we talk, we deliver, and hardly break a sweat doing any of it. Due to the industry being in its infancy stages, there is a complexity that is innate to wild west nature attached to the industry. Product sales are negotiated with tentative terms, one moment you have a buyer or have found product for purchase; then the day of the sale, they will say that they would like to purchase the product on terms (Not COD), or a different buyer paying more has come in and purchased what they have already agreed to sell to you.

The world of Cannabis sales is filled with daily unknowns, but with a little bit of faith and optimism, you can be excited about the sales opportunities that are sure to come your way through the product you have on hand or product you have access to. Fitting your product piece with your buyer's product need is how you will create your sales. If the product doesn't match what they are searching for, then you have the wrong piece.

Essentially, we are master puzzle masters aligning people and products to create opportunities for our customers and ourselves. Farmers and dispensaries have different needs and different wants and rarely do they discuss them with each other. It is up to us to put the farmers wants with the dispensary's needs. In the world of the sales rep, opportunity floats around us all the time. It is up to us to see the daily opportunities that are possible and align the correct pieces (buyers and sellers) that make complete the sale.

In the beginning, you will be working with a limited number of puzzle pieces. You may have two items to sell and one consistent buyer on your board. But as you expand the brands you represent and grow the customers that buy from you, you will start to notice that you are working on a 5000-piece puzzle and the abundance of sales opportunities are more than you can even take advantage of. It will be up to you to discern which pieces go where. Lining up the right pieces means sales. Just like a table puzzle, you may try a piece that doesn't fit. You put it back and try a different piece until you find one that does fit.

The largest puzzle pieces I ever connected, was between me and a seller that was selling three cannabis businesses for $900,000. Little did I know that this puzzle piece that was presented to me, that I would be the connecting piece, connecting these pieces lead me to becoming the owner of Lifted Northwest the dispensary, wholesale, and processing company.

In September of 2020 I was approached by a good friend that I had known professionally in the industry for the last four years, he had watched me grow since I entered the industry and knew that I was connected to lots of people in and outside our industry. One day he called me and asked if I would help him find a buyer for three licenses that were owned by the same company and that all the licenses where in the same building, he explained that there was an already active and functioning dispensary, wholesale, and processing license and all three needed to be sold as a package. Knowing I was always hungry for sales he informed me that there would be a finder's fee paid to me once the deal was complete, with a 10K possible payment looming, this deal quickly shot to the top of my priority list. First, I broke down the deal to figure out its selling points, what are the sales numbers? Are the licenses within the same building? Is the 1 million dollar purchase able to be negotiated on terms?

For the next two weeks I called everyone I knew in state and out of state, telling them how much of a great deal it was. The dispensary is already up and making money and the two other licenses are located within the same building, the building is leased out for the next ten years and happens to be in a very busy part of town. Just like any deal that I had tried to piece together before, there was push back and requests for different terms. Will the seller come done to $900K? How about $850? How much of a down payment would they be willing to accept to hold the deal? Will they allow us to pay them the purchase amount in several lump sums over a year? After two weeks' time, I was still unable to find a buyer; then one day it me.

I am the other piece of this deal.

At the time I had been searching for my own whole-sale and had not even considered the one right in front of me; I almost let the fear of the price keep me from recognizing the opportunity in my hands. I had been searching for a buyer, reconfiguring the deal for different people; then recognized that I had been creating the perfect deal for me and my team.

This book is not an end-all tell-all to Cannabis sales. I don't know everything there is to know as I am learning every day and will surely create some revisions to this book on cannabis sales. But for now, this is what I have learned over my five years in the recreational industry and what has helped me grow from sales rep to business owner.

I hope you become a great cannabis sales rep and make a book that adds to the knowledge we have in this exciting space of the legal Cannabis industry. Though I have laid out some solid advice and information in this book, the true learning will come from learning from your own experiences.

"Only a fool learns from his own mistakes, the wise man also learns from the mistakes of others – Otto von Bismark".

Mistakes will happen, be excited about your mistakes as they are probably mistakes you have never encountered before, and that equals growth! Use this guide to navigate around some of the potholes of misfortune and lead yourself to the financial prosperity found in the industry filled with Green Gold.

Sales Hack: Don't count yourself out- It took me a few weeks to see that the deal I was trying to connect someone else to was for me, the thought that I was the missing puzzle piece didn't even enter my mind. Yes, this book is about sales, and when you start you will probably be working for someone, but keep your entrepreneur eyes open, your business owner opportunity is just around the corner.

Sales Hack: Not your deal, not your product, still your money- Everyone and everything is a puzzle piece in this industry, you must be able to see with the eyes of a puzzle master. Sometimes you will sell someone's product for them, sometimes other sales reps can sell your product for you. Never close your eyes on a deal or how it can be worked, even if you only get a piece of a deal, that will keep your deal momentum rolling, and don't let greed get in the way of you making a deal. There is allot more earned in helping a deal go through than money. Don't forget that relationships are the way to the deal, soon people will think of you when they have a puzzle piece, next thing you know deals are coming at you from multiple people and you are connecting puzzle pieces on multiple puzzle boards.

My Sales Strategies

Sales is akin to war, and in war, you must have a strategy if you are going to win! Sales is no different. Over the last 4 years, I have come up with different sales strategies that have helped me win in the sales war. Below, I have listed the strategies that I have employed to get larger and more consistent sales.

The 1st sale discount- The first sale is all about making the customer comfortable about their purchase and ensuing them that this product will do great in their shop. They must know that you will be there to take care of all their needs when it comes to having support behind your product. There is no better way to offer reassurance around an initial buy than by offering a first-time sale discount for their first purchase. You will need to verify that this is an option with the company you represent before proposing it to your customer, but if you are given the green light; this will be a great strategy to open doors, especially in a crowded market.

One pound a day- In the beginning, sales will be scattered and inconsistent, and it is easy to think this isn't working and that you will never make a lot of money doing this. But if you can dial your sights into selling 1lb/ day- or 10 units/ day, then soon selling one a day will become easy, and then you can work up to two /day. In the beginning, you want to just focus on crawling. The walking and sprinting will come.

Selling half lbs = more strains = more shelf real estate- The inside of the dispensary should be viewed as land to be conquered, real estate to be claimed. Whatever realm your product lies in will be your territory and your battle-field. You want to gain ground in your space by taking up as much room as they will allow. You can strategically do this by getting as many strains/varieties of your product on the shelf as possible. You can achieve this with flower by selling the dispensary half lbs instead of whole lbs, which in turn will allow you to occupy more jars/real-estate.

The Bulk Buy- Figure out the volume price breakpoint. Usually if a certain volume is purchased companies will come down on their price in order to sell more product in a single sale. Know those volume points, and don't be afraid to think outside of the price point previously given. I never thought of selling 100lbs at once until a dispensary asked if my company would be interested in a large volume purchase. After that all I wanted to do was sell lbs in 100lb increments. If you sell 100lbs @ $500/lb, that equals $50,000 if your commission rate is 10%- you just made $5k in a single day.

Multiple birds with one stone, selling to dispensary chains- What's better than selling to one dispensary? Selling to multiple dispensaries at once! You can achieve this by going after dispensary chains! Most dispensary chains prefer to buy in bulk (due to discount, apply the above strategy) and offer the same product throughout all their shops. Each dispensary chain has a main purchaser, and they will be at the purchasing location. Go after the purchaser for all the shops, and you can get into 3-5 dispensaries at one time.

Bring your lunch and get out of your car to eat- Being a Cannabis sales rep means that you are on the go ALL the TIME. If you don't bring a lunch, you will run into two problems. 1. Rushing from one account to the next, more times than not, you will forget or not make time to eat. 2. Eating out every day is VERY expensive. I have spent over $900 in one month dining out to lunch and dinner every day.

There is a lot to be said about enjoying your meal, and I think you must make time for yourself as a sales rep, it's too easy not to. So, each day, I make sure that I eat my lunch outside my car, at a beautiful park, or on top of the hood of the car in front of a field or river. Somewhere you can slow down for a minute and smell the roses, look at the scenery and be thankful to be alive and selling weed.

Be at your first shop 1 hour after They open, not the minute they open- How does it feel when someone at work is in your face asking for things before you have fully grasped what the day entails? Then I don't suggest going to a dispensary right when they open. Opening a dispensary in the morning consists of quite a few tasks, and usually they open with a limited number of staff. Let them open, let a few more budtenders trickle in; you will set yourself up for a person who has the time to step away and give your sale the attention it deserves.

Tread carefully when selling to Dispensaries in the same neighborhood- I have never let the proximity of physical location deter me from selling to a dispensary right down the street from another. But you must certainly be careful of what you sell and for how much. Generally, I try not to sell customers the same products that are right down the street from each other, it's not unheard of for a dispensary to send scouts to the nearby shops and see if you are selling product there and at what price. If a shop catches wind you have sold the same product to a nearby competitor, you better be sure to have sold them both the product at the same price. Any major differences in price will get you questioned and a bunch of drama you don't want.

Sell Everything- The more diversity you have in your product portfolio, the more options and possibilities you have for getting into a shop. The strategy here is to become a one-stop shop. At one point, I was selling cartridges, edibles, extracts, and selling flower. With this strategy, all you need to figure out is what/ where their product needs are and build the rapport. Next thing you know, you will be selling them a little of everything from each product line.

Go until you get the sale- Sales is all about running the numbers, and you must keep this at the forefront of your mind. You can only get a no or rejection so many times in a row; your yes is right around the corner. In the beginning, I would stay in the sales field until I got a sale, even if that meant visiting dispensaries around five or six pm (the later it gets, the less chance you will meet with the purchaser. I never let the lateness of the day discourage me. It just seemed to work out; go until you get the sale! I started to notice that for every 8-9 dispensaries I visited for sales, I would get a yes or at least a date when they would be ready to buy.

Buy your own product- This little trick is a way to deplete your product stock on a dispensaries shelf and also get it into the hands of the bud tenders. Since we know how imperative it is to get samples into the hands of the bud-tenders, why not buy it for them? I have walked into a dispensary and purchased my product for every budtender on the sales floor, directly from the dispensary shelf. Doing this accomplished a few things. 1- lowered the amount product left on the shelf. 2- Put samples directly into the hands of the people who sell my product. 3- Built up my value to them, this is not something that anyone ever does, so this action stands out in their minds; now when customers ask for products like mine; they will present mine first.

Bud Tender Challenges- Unfortunately bud tenders don't get paid that much, but you can capitalize on this economic misfortune by offering them incentives for selling your product. First you must speak with the sales director/ owner in your company and come up with the best offering to incentivize the bud tenders that sell your product. Sometimes its lunches, free product, tickets to a game, or good ol hard cash. The next step is to get the dispensary on board. You will have to speak with upper management to see if this fits their model of inside sales/ if they have the means to tracking who sells your product. If they can track who sells individual product, you will have to verify what prizes they deem appropriate for winning. Once all of this is lined up, you should have your company create some type of poster that outlines all the details of the challenge, when it starts, what's at stake, how they can win, and when the challenge ends; this should be hung in their brake room. With the right incentives you should see a spike in sales within the dispensary, which should lead to more sales to the dispensary.

This approach can be tweaked to provide a prize if an entire dispensary hits a certain sales goal, or as a challenge amongst dispensaries within a chain.

Use the state as your entire sales territory- Depending on how many sales reps your company has; you could be leaving thousands of commission dollars on the table each month. If you can expand your territory, you should create a plan of attack and hit the road. Small towns and outlying areas are often shown a lot less product than the larger cities, and therefore appreciate when new products come their way. There are gold mines/ big buyers just waiting to be discovered. Break outside your normal sales box and make the entire state your territory.

RECOMMENDED READINGS & AUDIO
Audio Books and public figures that helped refine me as a sales rep-

Rich Dad Poor Dad by **Robert Kiyosaki**
Be Obsessed or Be Average- by **Grant Cardone- This is my sales bible**
The 10x rule- by **Grant Cardone**
Ninja Selling- by **Larry Kendall**
The Power of Now- by **Eckart Tole**

The Untethered Soul- by **Michael A Singer**
The art of war plus the art of sales- by **Gary Gagliardi**
Lead the Field- by **Earl Nightingale**
The War of Art- by **Steven Pressfield**

Speeches and audios from-
Jim Rohn, Les Brown, Eric Thomas, Andy Frusella, David Goggins, CT Fletcher.

10 Weed sales Commandments

1. **Never get high on your own supply.**
2. **Wake up early- Being in sales will eat up your entire day. Waking up early to get the things done that mean the most to you is essential. I wrote this book by creating time, there is no time after 8am; the sales day has begun and I'm too tired at the end of the sale day. I had to force myself to start waking up at five and six AM to get as much writing in as possible before the sales day started. There is a quote that says, "The man who works all day, does not have time to make money" If you have other goals and ambitions, prioritize them by making them the first thing you do in your day!**
3. **Save your judgements for your friends- Never point out or say anything negative about an intake managers flower or product purchase. To make fun or dis the purchase is to make fun and dis the purchaser and their decision making, if they**

feel disrespected by you; then you have damaged one of the most important sales pieces- the relationship.

4. Don't burn bridges- The industry might seem big, but word of mouth travels the industry fast. Be kind, claim your mistakes, rectify all issues, and keep your reputation clean.

5. 80/20 Rule- give the shops that pay you the most money, the most time. If they love you, they will buy from you. Strong relationships require time and attention.

6. Be the energy- deliver more than the product! Deliver a mood! A smile!! Deliver the best part of their day, and you will continue to deliver. People have told me I have Benergy and that they love working with me; similar product can be found anywhere, my energy can't.

7. Always test your level of commitment to the passion- Do every out-of-the-ordinary thing that comes to your mind. Drive to the town 6 hours away! Pop into random shops without a heads up, help another company without thought of compensation. Jump at every opportunity to prove yourself to yourself, do this and opportunities will seem to pop up out of thin air.

8. Know your worth and learn to expand- Your relationships are everything! A good relationship with the purchaser means you have close to guaranteed sales in a shop, sales = income. If you are

good at what you do, you will have anywhere from 5-200+ relationships. Once there, it will be time to support many product producers.

9. **It's not all about you- Don't forget to show your accounts love outside of what you bring them. Show your appreciation with snacks, lunch, tickets to a game, samples, etc.. Don't be the guy who just shows up and always wants something. You look like a damn beggar.**

10. **Have a fucking ton of fun while you learn- This shouldn't feel like work all the time, and if you love it enough; it hardly will.**
    Always remember, you're legally selling weed.

Know the Lingo and Speak with Confidence

4/20- April the 20th (5 days away as I write this book!) National weed holiday!! Lots of sales opportunities in dispensaries the week prior and the days after. (Unless you are doing a vendor day/ meet and greet with customers; do not go to the shop for daily sales) The shops will be packed to the gills and will have prepared for major sales on this day. Let them sell. Stay out of the way!

7/10- If you type this into a calculator, it spells out OIL. On 7/10, dispensaries will usually make big sales on all extracts and cartridges. It's really just an excuse to throw some big sales and get people in the shops.

BCC- Blind Carbon Copy- You had better use this when

casting a net email. If you CC everyone, then everyone who receives the email will see who else the email was sent. They are usually competitors. Let's just say, you won't get any good replies.

BHO= Butane Hash Oil- Extraction process that uses Butane as the solvent/ separator.

Bud Tender- Front line employee in dispensaries that offer guidance to customers that come in, similar to a bartender. They will provide suggestions with and their personal opinion on the products within the shop.

Batter and budder: Terms that are used to describe the appearance of cannabis extracts. Batter or badder has the look and feel of frosting and usually has a soft, golden color. Budder's look is like actual butter and has a much softer texture

Calculating price per gram for off-weight LBs- This formula will allow you to calculate how much a bag of flower will cost if it is not in a full lb, for example- 157g, 265g, 430g. In order to calculate how much a bag of weight flower will cost, we must first know how much the Lb costs when it is full and then must divide that cost by how many grams are in a full lb (454g) once you have done this you have figured out how much each individual gram cost; multiply this number by the grams you have on hand, and you have calculated the cost of your off weight Lb.

Example- A dispensary is looking to purchase one of your lbs that weighs 329g, and the cost of the full lb is $1500. You would first divide 1500/454 to figure out the cost of each individual gram in a full lb which = $3.30 (454x$3.30=$1498- Round up to $1500). Since we know how much each gram costs, we have to multiply that gram price by how many grams we have in the bag we are selling. $3.30 x 329g=$1,085.7. A bag of flower that should be sold at $1500 for a full lb can be sold at $1,085.70 if it is only 329g.

Price of the full Lb $1500/ by the weight of a full lb 454g = Gram price $3.30. Gram price$3.30 multiplied by actual weight on hand = The price you would charge for an off weight lb). $1500/454 = $3.30 x 329g= $1,085.70lb

Cannabis medical Patient- A person who has an ailment that has seen a physician and has been deemed to have a chronic illness. With the proper paperwork filled out, they receive a medical card and usually have different purchasing privileges within the dispensary.

CBD-The second most used cannabinoid found in the cannabis plant. CBD is an antagonist to THC and is non-psychoactive as it blocks the formation of 11-OH-THC and mitigates the psychoactive effects of THC.

Centralized Buying- This is a purchasing strategy that is performed by companies with multiple retail shops. Purchasing this way allows for the company to take advantage of discounts offered in bulk purchases. Usually, the company purchasing will have a central location/ wholesale where they store the bulk product until their separate retail shops need inventory.

COA- (Certificate of Analysis) This paperwork states all the scientific tests run on the cannabis product by the sanctioned laboratory to determine Cannabinoid content, toxic chemical content, and mold content.

COD- Cash on delivery or check on delivery- When the product is dropped, it is paid for same day.

Crumble- identified by its malleable texture that falls apart, or "crumbles", when handled.

Distillate- is a highly refined extract typically containing a cannabinoid potency exceeding 75%. The distillation process involves the use of solvents such as butane or alcohol or solventless extraction methods to produce gold to clear viscous liquid

Dab/dabbing: A method where a "dab" (small amount) of cannabis concentrate is placed on a preheated surface, creating concentrated cannabis vapor to be inhaled.

Delivery manifest- In states where cannabis delivery is legal, there are requirements for cannabis distributors or dispensaries to fill out a delivery manifest (shipping manifest). This must accurately reflect the inventory being transported and cannot be altered or voided at any point during transport.

Edible- Cannabis products that are orally consumed. These products can contain THC, CBD, or a combination of both. Common edible products include cookies, brownies, candies, gummies, chocolates, beverages, or homemade goods

Endocannabinoid system (ECS)- A group of receptors that make up a very complex regulatory system throughout the human brain, body, and central and peripheral nervous systems. ECS creates and maintains our body's internal stability (homeostasis) by adjusting the flow of neurotransmitters and regulating bodily functions, including appetite, sleep, emotion, and movement

Entourage effect- the combined effect of different compounds found in cannabis that work together as a whole to produce a greater effect than if working separately to produce separate effects

Extracts- Cannabis extracts are specific concentrates that are produced with the use of a solvent. Common solvents used for this include propane, butane, and ethanol. Types of cannabis extracts include crumble, wax, shatter, budder, live resin, etc.

Flower trifecta- This is when a lb or entire harvest has an amazing look, smell, and THC %. Example- A hand-trimmed lb, with a strong aroma and a THC level of 25% or more. If your flower packs this punch, you will be able to call your price!

Flower Mold- Just like in food, cannabis flower and products can get moldy. The flower can get moldy from the flower retaining too much water within the bud, and without proper aeration can create the perfect environment for mold to grow. Mold happens. Just be sure to use your supreme customer service skills to ensure they are taken care of.

Full LB- 454g v-456g- A lb should weigh 454g to be a full lb. Farmers have learned that as a bud cures over time, it tends to dry out and lose a bit of its water weight. This will cause the lb to be short a couple of grams within a few weeks' time. Some farmers (Not all) take this into account and will weigh their lbs out to 456g so that when the drying occurs, it dries down to the weight it should be. ** Don't be afraid to weigh out your lbs if they have sat for a few weeks. If you show up to sell 10 lbs and every bag is short 2 grams, the purchasing manager might look at you funny.

Full Spectrum- Often called whole plant extracts, maintain the full profile of the cannabis plant.

Hand trim- Trim job done by hand tends to be a more expensive way to trim your flower. Trimers can get paid anywhere from $120-$170/lb. Though spendy, hand trimming produces the most aesthetically looking buds.

Hybrid- This is a strain that has been genetically crossed with the two opposing "types" of high, truthfully speaking, the strain has a close to 50/50 expression of opposing terpenes (myrcene + linalool).

Half Lb- 227-228g

The BM or Black market: includes all sellers of marijuana products that are doing so illegally. This could be a store that is not properly licensed in a legal state or a dealer that is selling cannabis illegally to consumers in legal or not legal markets, therefore avoiding regulations, taxes.

Indica- In-da-couch. – Classic descriptor of the sensation brought on by strains known to relax the body. It is now known that the responsible culprit for giving the body the relaxing feeling stems from the Terpenes present in the flower. Ex- Flowers with high linalool content are going to be more sedative; linalool 1

Intake Manager/ Purchasing manager- This is the purchaser and inventory keeper at the dispensary. This is the individual you will need to get in front of to sell into a shop.

Isolate: pure white, crystalline powder exceeding 98% for one individual cannabinoid. Through the refining process, all organic plant matter such as waxes, chlorophyll and plant oils have been removed.

Kief: also known as pollen or dry sift, refers to the resin glands which contain the terpenes and cannabinoids from the marijuana plant.

Landrace strain- refers to a local variety of cannabis that has adapted to the environment of its geographic location. This accounts for genetic variation between landrace strains, which have been crossbred to produce the cannabis variety we see today.

Laboratory- This is the quality control part of the industry, every product created for human consumption in the recreational industry must go through this checking process. It ensures harmful and toxic chemicals are not present in the products being sold in the dispensaries.

Light Dep- Also stands for light deprived. This is a growing technique to trick plants into budding earlier than if they had allowed the seasons to pass naturally. This technique is primarily used in outdoor growing and allows the farmer to produce more than one harvest in the same year. By depriving the light from the plants during certain time periods, the farmer is mimicking the changing of the seasons; tricking the plants into thinking that summer has passed and its time to start budding.

Live Resin- When a cannabis concentrate is made using freshly picked plants that are immediately harvested and frozen, the product is known as live resin

Living soil- is a planting strategy used for cannabis that has active microbiology and biodiversity within the soil medium. This may include worms, bacteria, protozoa, amoebas, and kelp extracts. This type of cultivation technique is considered healthier and safer than standard soil use because it helps eliminate the need for fertilizers and bottled nutrients

Machine trim- Trimming done by a machine usually tumbles the buds around in a tube with blades through the sides. This is a bit rough on the buds and tends to knock off quite a bit of the Trichomes. It also leaves what we call a "loose trim job," meaning there is quite a bit of leaf still left on the bud, greatly taking away from the look if it is left to be sold this way.

Manifest- Paperwork that shows the exact turn by turn directions from the originating facility to the destination of the product being transported from one cannabis-approved location to another. The manifest also provides the vehicle make and model, along with the Driver's license number, plate, name, and phone number of the driver doing the transporting. This is the paperwork that makes you legal, and if you are ever pulled over and questioned by the police- your saving grace.

OG – Doesn't come from the acronym original gangster, it is actually a term that originated to describe Southern California's Ocean Grown Kush, due to the fact is was grown so close to the ocean.

Phenotype- a term that is heard most often in growing. It refers to the general physical characteristics of the plant such as height, color, branching, leaf configuration down to cell structure

Non-compliance: in the cannabis industry means that a marijuana business is not in compliance with specific state or local laws. The business will be at risk of penalties from either the state or local government which include but are not limited to, fines, revoking of a license, or other consequences

Pesticide: Chemical or organic substances that might be used on cannabis plants to protect against insects and/or fungus. Due to the Schedule I status of cannabis, as well as the lack of research and understanding, there are no federal regulations on the application of pesticides on cannabis

PHO= Propane Hash Oil- The extraction process uses propane as the solvent/ separator. A cheaper way to separate the trichomes from the plant material during the extraction process.

Producer- also known as the grower and or farmer. They grow the weed and either hire a wholesaler to sell their flower, or a salesman.

Processor- This is the extract maker! They make the dabs, cartridges, and other Value-added products made from the bud or trimmings of the cannabis plant.

Quarter LB- 113.5-114g

RSO or Rick Simpson Oil- is a cannabis concentrate created in 2003 by Rick Simpson to treat his basal cell carcinoma. **RSO** is widely used for medical benefits and has been found to relieve cancer symptoms

Seed-to-sale- Everything that happens to an individual cannabis plant from seed and cultivation, through growth, harvest, and preparation of cannabis-infused products, if any, to final sale of finished products

Shake- The bottom of your bag after nugs have been broken up and in a bag for a little bit. Also, the bottom of the jar in a dispensary. ***Hack- This is where all the THC falls and can be quite tasty

Shatter- is a cannabis extract that is typically made through butane extraction

Solventless- Cannabis extract product made without the use of solvents or chemicals.

Terms- Agreed upon the amount of time that the dispensary may have the product without yielding payment. Usually in a 7,14,30 daytime allotment.

Terpenes- Fragrant oils secreted from the resin glands of flowers that provide aromatic diversity. They are not just found in the cannabis plant, but other plants as well. Terpenes bind to different receptors in the brain to give different effects

Tincture- A liquid form of cannabis that is made from glycerine or alcohol. Tinctures are usually distributed in an eyedropper under the tongue to provide fast absorption to the body, leading to quicker effects than edibles and inhalation
Topical- Topicals are cannabis-infused lotions, oils, and balms that users apply directly to the skin for pain and inflammation relief. Cannabis topicals are non-intoxicating so the user can experience the medicinal properties of cannabis without the psychoactive effects.

Total Cannabinoid content v THC Content- When Cannabis products are tested for THC potency, they are also tested for the other Cannabinoids present.

Trichome- Also known as crystals, trichomes are resin-producing glands on a marijuana plant. They have the appearance of small hairs. Trichomes are responsible for producing the large majority of a cannabis plant's cannabinoids

Trim- When the plant has been harvested, a grower will trim the plant of its leaves, placing focus on the remaining buds

THC-. Delta-9-tetrahydrocannabinol (THC) is a cannabinoid found in cannabis. THC is the most well-known molecule in marijuana and is sought after for its euphoric, psychological effects

Tincture: Cannabis tinctures are made by infusing cannabis with alcohol. They are often used for medicinal purposes, are taken orally, and can contain high levels of both THC and CBD

Top Shelf: Similar to how liquor stores display the highest quality products on the top shelf, top shelf is an expression often used in cannabis dispensaries to highlight high-quality products being sold

Vendor Day- Pre-organized time and date set by the dispensary and vendor- usually a 2-4 hr event. Cantered around a deal or offer of swag from the vendor- Representative from the vendor company

Vertical Integration- A company that provides or can provide their products for their shelves. In the Cannabis world, a vertically integrated company would produce their own flower, extracts, edibles, cartridges; and sell them in their own shop. This is one of my first questions when I walk into a new dispensary, it immediately helps me uncover if they bring in a ton of their own products, and if so which ones? or if they supply their shelves by mainly purchasing from farms and wholesalers.

Water Weight- The weight held onto by freshly harvested flower. Over time this weight sill be lost due to drying, the longer a bud is separated from the plant, the drier it will become. Most farmers will weigh their bags to a few grams less than the presented weight. This allows for drying and the loss of water weight, leaving the dried product to be right at or very close to the weight after some time has passed.

Wholesaler- This is the middleman that knows he can move certain product to certain shops, with speed! There are two ways wholesalers operate, they either purchase product at a discounted price and sell it for higher, or they sell directly for but independently of the farm; for a commission % previously agreed upon. Long story short, they sell a bunch of flowers for a bunch of different farms at once, and if they are selling for commissions, they don't get paid until they put the cash in the farmer's hands.

Growth= "If it scares you, then you already know; if it doesn't, then it's time to go."

About the Author

Benjamin has been in Cannabis industry for over 10 years, five in the illicit market and five in the legal recreational market. Getting into the legal recreational market is where he has grown his passion for Cannabis and business. In this short amount of time, he has grown his value to the Cannabis market from once only a sales rep, to now being one of the youngest owners of multiple cannabis licenses in Portland Oregon.

He and his business + life partner Amanda are the proud owners of the dispensary Lifted Northwest, where they employ over 19 employees throughout their production team, wholesale team, and dispensary staff.

At Lifted Northwest they are constantly pioneering new products and preparing for when they can bring Oregon Cannabis to the rest of the nation. They recently launched one of the only ten full gram pre roll packs in Oregon and are working on producing more products that have not yet been created.

They have also launched a clothing brand called Lifted Lifestyle where they produce smoking related items, unique ash trays, rolling trays, and smoker related apparel, along with Oregon inspired clothing apparel.

Made in the USA
Columbia, SC
05 August 2022

64380376R00108